GUYS AND GARAGES

Helena Day Breese

THE LYONS PRESS

Guilford, Connecticut

An Imprint of The Globe Pequot Press

The Lyons Press is an imprint of The Globe Pequot Press

All photos © Helena Day Breese except p. 103 by Mark Stucky
Text designed by Peter Holm, Sterling Hill Productions

Library of Congress Cataloging-in-Publication Data is available on file.
ISBN 978-0-7627-4443-5

Printed in China

10 9 8 7 6 5 4 3 2 1

For Rita and Alan
Who Made Me

HAPPY THE MAN

Happy the man, and happy he alone,
  He who can call today his own:
  He who, secure within, can say,
Tomorrow do thy worst, for I have lived today.
  Be fair or foul or rain or shine
The joys I have possessed, in spite of fate, are mine.
Not Heaven itself upon the past has power,
But what has been, has been, and I have had my hour.

—John Dryden, 1631–1700

CONTENTS

Garage . . . Door Openers

I like to putter around the garage. I used to think that this was a sign of getting older, but I'm more convinced than ever that great things happen in garages. If you don't putter, it's not too late.

The first Apple computer was built in a garage. And the people who syndicate the Oprah Winfrey show started their concept in a garage. I have a good friend, right here in Indy, who started his multimillion dollar candy business in his tiny garage.

This has really begun to bug me. I have never started anything in my garage. Well, I did start my 1978 Ford Pinto when it was only thirty-five degrees. I should get some points for that. And let's see, I did start to clean the garage once. I never finished, so I can't take credit for that.

Of course, when you realize how many creative ideas originated in garages and how much money has been generated from people's garages, you wonder why parents still push the Wharton School of Business. I mean the cost of college tuition now exceeds $100,000 for four years. You can get a really decent garage for about a third of that and have it the rest of your life. I spent a total of seven years in college and never had an idea that was worth more than a couple of bucks. My mistake? Living in the dorm, of course.

What kills me is how many times my very own father said to me, "Sure you can come home and live after college, but you'll have to stay in the garage." I never really appreciated my father's wisdom until now.

I don't know what it is about garages. I have no recollection of reading about someone making an important discovery in his living room. And when's the last time someone said to you: "You know, I just had the greatest idea while up in my attic." And spare bedrooms? I don't think one earth-shattering accomplishment has ever been generated from a spare bedroom.

Even criminals love garages. You hear all the time how a terrorist built a bomb in his garage. But when's the last time that a killer planned his next murder in the sunroom? Or a bank robber charted his Brinks robbery on the screened-in patio? Garages just bring out the best in people.

Maybe it's the fumes. In my garage you get that wonderful mixture of gasoline, bug spray, and paint. Those chemical reactions go right to your brain and can result in a five-state killing spree or Oprah Winfrey on TV in 240 cities. Don't underestimate the power of a garage.

I sat in my garage the other day reflecting on all the time I've wasted at the beach contemplating Plato or in my bedroom listening to Mozart. And for what? Just so some computer geek could sit in the corner of his garage straddling a lawnmower and make billions of dollars.

So if you like to putter around your garage, do it with your head held high. Just don't trip over the snowblower.

—DICK WOLFSIE

Author of 67 Ways to Amuse Yourself in Two Minutes or Less

ACKNOWLEDGMENTS

I am deeply indebted to all my friends for their generosity and support while I researched and wrote this book. Special thanks are due to Don Mills, for the many life-sustaining lunches spent scheming ideas together and for everything he did to help me succeed with this one; to Marty Good, who believes all things are possible; to Dolores Nyerges for her encouragement; to Christopher Nyerges, my agent, for finding me a publisher; to Jennifer Kantor, for always being there for me from the start to the "finish line"; and to Mark Stucky for beach walks and laughter along the way. Thanks also to my dear family who bring immeasurable happiness to my life and who have supported all my endeavors from afar with love and enthusiasm.

I am also grateful to the following people, whose superb knowledge and skills helped me realize my vision: Sharon Nichols, the best copy editor a writer could ever wish for and whose ability to "understand" the guys without ever meeting them was a true gift to me; Glen Derbyshire for his experienced photographer's eye and expert photo editing, for teaching me to "see the light," and of course, for the beer; Carmen Smyth, for making the first road trip a success and for her energy, enthusiasm, and photographic assistance—many of the best shots I owe to you.

I further extend my thanks to everyone who contributed to the serendipitous process of finding guys and their garages with inspired suggestions, recommendations, and connections: Annie Dahlgren, for her enthusiasm at the very start of this project and for finding me my first guys; Kelsey, for sharing her extensive e-mail list; Meryl Weider, Carmen Porto, Jonathon Talbot, Jeff Marshall and Geiger for introducing me to friends with garages when I thought the well was running dry; and Kathy Hickey, April James, Sandy Beisler, Julie Nelson, Deirdre O'Brien, Nancy Mitchell, Alan and Michelle Ludwick, Jen and Chip Winchell, Bob Pauls, and Ines and Gilbert Roberts for their warm hospitality.

I thank award-winning Indianapolis humor writer and news anchor Dick Wolfsie for contributing the foreword to this volume. His wit and clever observations provided a unique introduction to the book. I also thank Gillian Belnap, my editor at The Lyons Press, for sharing my vision and shepherding me through the book publishing process.

Most of all, I am indebted to all the guys I interviewed and photographed not only for opening their garage doors to me, but also their hearts. Without you, this book would never have been possible.

GUYS AND GARAGES

BILL W.

Bill is a "bug man." No, he doesn't exterminate household pests; he is a man dedicated to finding discarded, dilapidated Volkswagen Beetles and restoring them to their former glory.

Bill's love affair with cars goes way back. He started his first hot rod club, the Camtwisters of Greene, as a teenager in his parents' garage. Now, many years later, he's still a hot rod and vintage car enthusiast. In fact, every year he drives his 1973 Wolfsburg VW up to the Watkins Glen Racetrack, some seventy-five miles away, and camps overnight in his Beetle so he can relish every minute of the huge vintage car event they hold there.

Back at home, the garage where Bill gives new life to his beloved VWs may seem an unusual place to perform such modern feats of magic. First, the space is extremely small, and second, it resembles a nineteenth-century carriage house, more suited to sheltering an old-fashioned buggy and high-stepping horse than the Volkswagens that actually live there. But Bill has found a way to make it all work. With one of his cars parked inside, he has just enough "squeeze room" to make his way to a small alcove in the back where he has set up a comfortable stool, a good light to work by, and all of his tools within easy reach.

Over the years in his garage, Bill has saved many a VW from an ignominious end in a lonely junkyard. "I look for really challenging cars for my projects," he says. Then he laughs as he points to the 1973 Beetle that currently occupies the garage. "My wife told me I couldn't buy this one if it came in pieces. Sure enough, it arrived in a bunch of boxes!"

Bill got to keep his project, though—partly because his wife has a soft heart and maybe partly because he is not the only one in the family with the VW "bug." His son drives a Jetta, and his wife loves her Volkswagen Passat. And, it might also have something to do with the fact that Bill moves his projects out of the garage all winter so his wife's Passat can stay warm and dry.

"It's my summer garage."

HEATH

When Heath's wife told him the garage was "all his," he was a happy man. That's because he knew exactly what he was going to do with it. And it wasn't going to be used just for parking a car and storing a few tools.

What Heath created was a stylish space that not only functions as a garage but also serves as his office and playroom. It's set up with a desk, sofa, and surround-sound TV, and on the floor he's placed a gigantic cushion for his three lovable dogs, Iggy, Vicious, and Grohl. "When I'm in my garage," Health explains, "I feel comfortable and inspired because I get to be surrounded by the things I love—my bikes, my monsters, my tools, my music, my movies, and my dogs."

You might have already guessed that Heath is a collector. One of his collections involves monsters—Frankenstein in particular. He also collects anything having to do with James Dean and proudly displays his fine photographs of the movie star, many of which came directly from the Indiana James Dean Museum when it closed down. "Every year I attend the annual James Dean event in his hometown of Fairmount, Indiana," Heath says. "And I always visit his grave site when I'm there."

"My business and my lifestyle are one," Heath continues. And he has just the style and artistic ability to make such disparate themes really work together—the vintage motorcycle jackets and rockabilly- and tattoo-inspired clothing that he sells blend seamlessly with his modern art, his monster collection, and all his other toys.

According to Heath, the space "still functions as a garage, too," and he does indeed have a KX 125 Kawasaki dirt bike and a black Triumph Bonneville motorcycle parked against one wall. In Heath's garage, though, these vehicles seem to add to the stylishness of the space rather than making it feel more conventional. And when he opens the drawers of his red metal toolbox, a treasure trove of Triumph memorabilia is discovered—old Triumph patches from the 1970s, Indy 500 patches, and Triumph mirrors—in addition to a single drawer containing practical tools.

So, does Heath's wife ever wander over to his garage? "Oh yes!" he says. "When she visits we have wine and relax and watch a movie." Then he adds, "It's like there's an extra room in our house—only it's all mine!"

"My wife gave me the garage!"

CHIP, ALAN, AND CLYDE

Like clockwork, every Tuesday around dinnertime Chip, Alan, and Clyde congregate in Alan's garage for an evening of decompression and male culture. As Chip puts it, "Working on cars is a great stress reliever." And this team has the de-stressing routine down pat.

First, Alan fires up the "hubcap barbie" behind his garage and, while the hamburgers sizzle, the first round of cold beers comes out. After the guys put the burgers away, the action moves around to the front of the garage, where more beers are consumed, cigars are lit, and a friendly and leisurely exchange of news and views begins. Clyde explains the process: "We scratch, we grunt, and we tell lies—and each week the lies get bigger!"

With the cigars gone and night falling, there is only one thing left to do: get a bit of work done on "the car," the 1976 Porsche 911 body that's currently suspended in midair on a rotisserie stand inside Alan's garage. Of course, the guys feel a rotisserie stand is a necessary device for a team effort like this. As Clyde points out, "You only have so many bend-overs in a lifetime, and we're making sure our allotment lasts as long as possible."

Once in a while, though, Testosterone Tuesdays can get exciting, such as the time the guys, frustrated with the tedious process of scraping away the car's old insulation material, decided to use a blowtorch to "soften and assist the removal." The resulting fire might have engulfed the entire car had it not been for the team's rapid response and their quick-thinking switch from using their scrapers as scrapers to using their scrapers as fire dampeners. "What do you expect?" asks Chip with a shrug. "It's Alan's garage, and we're just cheap labor, after all."

But there is a general plan—"a natural progression," as Alan calls it. "We're stripping paint and adding roll bars while the engine is off being overhauled by a local Porsche specialist." And, eventually, Alan will race the Porsche in Florida SCCA events at Daytona and Sebring International Raceway.

Dirty, happy, and ready to call it a night, the fraternity eventually disbands for the week. Chip takes off on what Clyde calls a "retro rod"—his 1973 Triumph Bonneville—and Clyde jumps into his truck and drives away. Meanwhile, Alan locks up the garage and strolls back into the house. Testosterone Tuesday comes to a close.

"We call it Testosterone Tuesday."

BARNEY

Some artists work in oils, others in watercolors. But there is probably only one artist in the world who works in toilet seats: Barney Smith.

It was an inspired moment, now some thirty-five years ago, when Barney discovered his unique medium. "My dad and I were both retired master plumbers, and we returned home from a deer hunt with small bucks. I mounted my antlers on a toilet seat lid," says Barney. "Since then I have mounted deer horns, hides, and turkey feathers from our hunts and also other things such as a piece of the Berlin Wall, a bit of Mount St. Helens volcanic ash, and other historic artifacts."

"I now have 808 exhibits hung in my garage, and it takes about twenty hours to complete one," Barney continues, which means he has spent a lot of time in his garage. "If I'm not in the house, my wife always knows where I am!" he laughs.

But Barney's art might never have come to light had it not been for the encouragement of a fellow artist. "I took him to look at some oil paintings hanging in the garage along with the toilet seats, and he let the cat out of the bag! He contacted a local TV station." After that, Barney decided to put his art on view and opened his cavernous four-car garage to the public.

Barney works with "found" materials—his first plaques were made from some damaged seats he came across at a local plumbing supply store. "I like to show the world that nothing needs to be thrown away," he explains. "I take the hinges off and use both parts of the seat." People from all over the world send Barney different things they think he might be able to use in his art. "And when they do," he says, "I engrave their names on the backside."

Some of Barney's creations have a very personal meaning for him, too. "I've set aside my 800th seat to decorate on my eighty-sixth birthday," he says. And one of his favorites is his "Tree of Life," a strong tree trunk design that symbolizes his long marriage to Velma. "Our initials are carved in the trunk, and there are three limbs for our daughters, seven limbs for our grandchildren, and eleven twigs for our great-grandchildren with their names inscribed on the back."

Barney opens his Texas garage museum nearly every day and hangs out his sign; appropriately, it's a simply painted toilet seat announcing "Art Museum—Welcome—No Charge. Barney Smith Artist." Over a thousand people find him annually, and his overflowing guest books record visitors from some sixty-one countries. "I would open my garage at midnight if I knew you were coming," he says.

"After I retired,

I thought I would stick with my trade."

ED

Ed has spent just about every day of his life working on one of the cars in one of his many garages. In fact, his now-grown daughter says her earliest, and fondest, memory is of crawling underneath one of those cars just to hang out with her dad. Fixing cars is what Ed does—and what he will always do. Today he's working on his 1966 Chevy Nova, one of the six projects he has scattered around his property. His favorite country radio station is playing softly in the background. "As soon as I finish one," says Ed, "I just go out in the yard and get me another."

Ed's forte is bodywork. He can take a wrecked car body that's been crumpled up like a piece of paper and turn it back into the gleaming vision that was driven out of the showroom. He works at a steady, measured pace, to very high standards. "I'm a perfectionist," says Ed, but his high standards have been both a blessing and a curse.

Ed used to work at an auto body shop. He was happy there, and his skills were appreciated by his many satisfied customers. But the shop became unionized, and Ed's working speed was deemed far too slow by union standards. He refused to rush his work, though, and produce what he considered substandard results. So at the age of fifty-eight, he decided to call it quits instead.

It wasn't an easy decision for Ed to make, but he chose—wisely, it turns out—to just continue what he did best, only out of the house. Slowly he built up a good customer base and, over time, his business blossomed. Indeed, as he's run out of space he's had to be creative, constructing a number of garages around his property. The first one came attached to the house, two are garage "tents," and the other is an additional four-car garage he built behind the house.

Ed says he's retired now, but it's hard to tell that by his workload. He has several longtime buddies who drop by often to work on his Chevys with him, and among them they can make any missing part and get any Chevy up and running again. In fact, Ed's daughter says nothing's really changed—she still has to go stick her head under the car to find out what her dad is up to.

"It's better than sitting in front of the TV!"

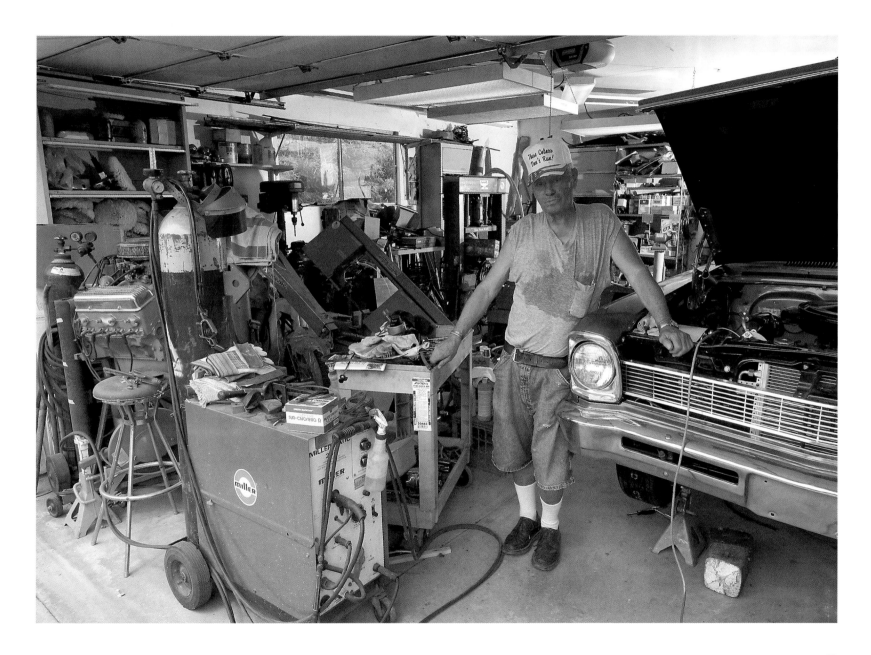

DALE

Though Dale has had his garage for thirty years, it looks nothing like it did when he got it. He's enlarged it by adding a couple of wings on the sides and installing several new windows. With this expansion he's been able—just barely—to keep up with the ever-growing collection of equipment necessary to his many life interests, namely fishing, sailing, black powder shooting, and the building and flying of model airplanes. But since his retirement it's the planes that take up most of Dale's garage space—and his time.

"I work on the planes every day—building them, flying them, crashing them, then fixing them again," he laughs. "Sandy loves it!" he says, glancing at his beloved dog, who, from the comfort of her garage bed, keeps a close eye on his activities all day long. "I just say the word flying and she's up, wagging her tail, ready for a trip up into the hills. She loves that!"

Dale has been building model planes since 1964. "Back then," he recalls, "my kids, along with all the other kids in the neighborhood, were really into it. And all the dads on the street spent their nights fixing the planes so we could all fly them by day. It was a fun time." He goes on to explain how the model planes were different back in those days. "We made them ourselves out of balsa wood, tissue paper, and glue. Now they're all made from plastic, molded foam, epoxy resin, and carbon fiber. And they all come from China as RTFs and ARFs." For the uninitiated, that's model plane lingo for "ready-to-fly" and "almost-ready-to-fly."

According to Dale, there are more model airplane enthusiasts now than ever before, since these days anybody can just go to Kmart and buy a "park flyer." A what? "It's called that because you just take it out of the box, park it, fly it, and crash it. Then you go buy another one!"

"I've made a few changes to my garage over the years."

But Dale still enjoys building and repairing the planes as much as he does flying them, which may explain all the spare wings and fuselages stashed in every corner of his garage.

And what about those kids, all grown up now, who used to enjoy flying with him—do they still do it? "Sometimes," says Dale. "And my grandson is into it now." The family tradition continues . . .

STEVE S.

Spending time in his garage has made Steve philosophical. Maybe it's because he's been working on projects there for more than thirty years. Or maybe it's the special project he's been working on every weekend for the last three and a half years: building wooden crosses for each American soldier whose life was lost in Iraq the previous week, for a memorial in his local town of Santa Barbara. "Whatever the reason," Steve says, "my garage is a place where I can let my mind wander while I work."

Steve's musings are all about life. "At fifty-nine years old, you realize that most of your life is behind you," he reflects. "Here's my garage philosophy on that: Life's like a bowl of ice cream. You may have eaten most of it, but there's still a lot left and it still tastes just as good as the first spoonful!"

Another musing has led him to the conclusion that "our lives are like garages . . . if we have the space, then we just fill it up." He laments, "When I was younger, I had time to grab my guitar and hang out with my friends. If I wanted to buy something, I'd save until I had the money. Now it seems that we rush into everything and our lives are so cluttered that all our spare time is gone."

Steve spends a lot more time these days asking "why," which has helped deepen his commitment to some of the things he cares about— like reducing his CO_2 footprint and dependence on fossil fuels. "You don't have to invade other people's countries to steal their sunshine," he says. It's not surprising, then, to learn that Steve generates his own electricity from domestic solar panels and has clean-fuel plans beyond that.

"Did you know that 85 percent of trips made in private automobiles are less than thirty miles long?" asks Steve. Pointing to a shiny new electric motor sitting in a box on his garage floor, he adds, "I'm working

on converting my 1969 VW bug to an electric car. When it's done, the family will use it for our trips around town, and instead of gasoline, we'll be driving around on sunshine!"

Turning his attention to the wooden crosses on his workbench, several that are returning for repair, he muses, "I feel I've gotten to know some of these so well, I should name them. My nine-year-old daughter does that—she names everything she loves."

"It takes me about four hours every Saturday to make them."

BARRY

Once upon a time, a modest garage was enough for Barry's restoration projects. But these days, faced with the gigantic task of bringing a 150-million-year-old brontosaurus (apatosaurus) back to life, Barry needs a "garage" the size of a 100-year-old Pennsylvania dairy barn.

How do you get from antique cars to dinosaurs? In Barry's case, it was a bit of luck: "I met my wife, April!" On their first date, Barry was inspired to explain how he had gotten sidetracked by car restoration even though his master's degree was in vertebrate paleontology. His lifelong dream was to take people on geological field trips. April was impressed. So, somewhere between appetizers and dessert, a business and a lifelong partnership were born.

Their "Prehistoric Journeys" field trips led to requests from museums for fossil preparation, which was accomplished in their single-car garage. "I've prepped and display-mounted 155 skeletons," Barry says, holding the tail of a 65-million-year-old sail-back edaphosaur skeleton that looks capable of walking off the bench and out the door.

But it's the apatosaurus, only the seventh one discovered and by far the most complete, that is Barry's biggest paleo project to date. The enormous bones, many still protectively wrapped in plaster jackets, occupy much of the barn's floor space. "Some of these fossilized bones weigh five hundred pounds or more," says Barry. "They arrived on moving vans that backed right into the barn!"

This dinosaur held an amazing surprise for Barry. "One night, I was working on bones in a plaster jacket when I recognized the distinctive shape of the brain case. Up to that point, there had never been an apatosaurus found with skull material directly related to the skeleton.

Although this is the biggest creature to have walked on Earth, the actual brain was smaller than an avocado. So, it was easy to wrap that brain case in a towel and carry it into the house to show April. She looked at the towel and whispered, 'You found skull bone!' It still gives me goose bumps when I think about the find. As a result of the brain case, this dinosaur is named Einstein."

When the skeleton is finished, Einstein will stand eighteen feet tall and stretch seventy feet long. "He'll just fit into our barn," Barry says, "with a few feet to spare when we close the door."

"I used to restore old cars,

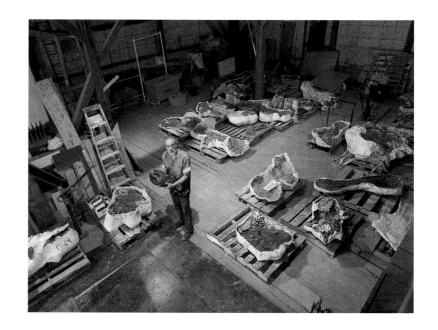

but now I revive dinosaurs."

STEVE M.

Steve's personal zeitgeist is "Follow your heart in life and see where it takes you." And in Steve's case, his heart has led him to two extraordinary careers. "I've been able to make a reasonable living both as a professional timpanist and as a chiropractor," he says. So it's not surprising to find that this man's garage truly mirrors his life. "I've set up my three-car garage so I can have a music studio and a light and airy chiropractic office where I see my patients, and I still have a personal area with space to store my motorcycles."

Music has always been a big part of Steve's life. "My parents started me young with violin lessons, but the violin just wasn't me," he says. "In fact, I found the instrument that was right for me in elementary school when my mother took me to a concert and I experienced the timpani [kettle drums] for the first time. But playing timpani at school wasn't all that cool, so my parents gave me a drum set instead. Much later I was able to become reacquainted with the timpani, and I knew immediately that I had been right so many years before—the timpani is my instrument." Nowadays, Steve's garage music studio is filled with gleaming copper kettle drums. "These have a marvelous sound," he says, tapping a pair made in the 1920s from calf skin.

"I became a chiropractor because the chiropractor I was seeing for treatment told me I would make a good one myself," Steve continues. "At the time, all I wanted to be was a musician. But later, when I realized how hard it was to make a living at it, I decided to follow her advice and go to chiropractic school." After thirty-five years in practice, he's never regretted that decision.

"I did my first chiropractic adjustment on my pet hamster, who was losing his hair," says Steve. "It was a great success," and for the budding chiropractor, the beginning of an unusual practice. "I've worked on as many animals as I have people over the years—from a goldfish that couldn't swim upright to horses—because if it works for people, it works for animals. Animals suffer just as we do, and I get a lot of satisfaction from relieving their pain."

As for the Harley, "Well, I picked that up on my birthday—it's such an American icon!" And, although he doesn't say on which birthday he got it, it seems to take years off him every time he rides—because, like all things Steve does in life, he does it with all his heart.

"My garage

allows me to express my three passions."

NEAL

Neal would love a bigger garage. "Since the house needs a new foundation anyway, if I had my way, I would jack it up, dig out all the dirt underneath, and have a full bottom-story garage. No garage would ever be big enough, though," he laments.

Crammed inside Neal's rustic 1930s garage are a partially dismantled 1955 MG TF 1500, a 1951 MGA 1600, and a 1941 Packard Super 8 limousine. A 1951 Chevy panel truck and a 1957 Morris Minor Woody, neither operational, seal the driveway. For Neal, moving the cars around to obtain some working space is like moving the plastic pieces in a slotted puzzle game. "My first step is to get a tow truck to move the panel truck that's blocking the garage door, and then, because the driveway slopes and the Packard is not drivable, the limo

has to be winched out of the garage on a cable. Then, with the Packard safely out of the way, I can get to my MGA." He cautions, however, that these maneuvers are best attempted when his wife is away for the weekend.

Neal describes himself as a "dismantler," able to turn any wrench counterclockwise but capable of making it go in the other direction only with great difficulty. Some thirty years ago such dismantling skills reduced his 1955 MG TF to a collection of disconnected parts when he attempted to replace a throw-out bearing. Removing the bearing was easy, so he thought he would just take the engine out and check it. Things, of course, went rapidly downhill from there. Neal had great plans for the MG at the time, but the car, owned by a mechanic devoid of "mantling" skills, never went back together again. Perhaps mercifully, his restoration plans for the 1951 Chevy truck now involve "preserving" the rust and decay, then buffing out the old layers of paint to decipher the tantalizing original signage that has just begun to appear.

Neal gets to visit his garage every weekend when he comes down to sweep it. "I like to turn a wrench or two," he says. "It makes me feel like I'm doing something—making progress." With five old cars, there is always something that needs doing, so Neal wisely keeps an operational 2003 Chevy Blazer parked on the street to run necessary errands.

"If I have an empty space, I fill it."

RON

Ron is film cameraman and member of the American Society of Cinematographers.

But he doesn't just shoot with cameras—he designs and builds equipment that makes challenging shots possible. So, if you need to figure out how to film a solar eclipse from a high-altitude plane or stabilize a camera on a powered paraglider to record ice floes in the Arctic, Ron's your man.

How does he do it? "My imagination works overtime to solve problems. If I haven't found a solution during the day, ideas often wake me in the middle of the night. They're my 'aha calls.'" And it's those "aha" wake-up calls that send Ron in search of the perfect object to do the job at hand—a quest that often leads to his garage to ferret out that long-stashed-away item he can modify after squeezing his way through the floor-to-ceiling equipment to his tiny workshop in the back. Toiling away in his little "cave," Ron says, is like therapy.

Ron shrugs off the staggering amount of equipment squirreled away in his garage. "What you see is the condensed version of what I once had. When I owned a commercial TV studio in Hollywood, I had two buildings full of gadgets." He learned the value of recycling and innovation at a young age. His father owned eighteen cabins at a mountain resort, and many evenings after finishing his vegetables, Ron would help his dad haul the guests' trash to "the dump," a treasures trove of other people's discards: Victrolas, radios, and other "good stuff."

Ron says that he "learned how things worked by taking them apart." And his dad had plenty of tools to work with—some he had actually made himself in his high school shop class. In this age of computer games, Ron wonders how many youngsters these days ever

get to learn by taking things apart with their own hands. "There's a tendency today for young people to not learn how things work, and this can cause problems when something needs fixing. When you're shooting on location, for example."

Ron has shot commercials in twenty-two countries and has surmounted the technical challenges posed by all. "I'm always well prepared," he says, then adds with a chuckle, "but sometimes the greatest challenges don't even involve the equipment—like the time in Mombassa when we were trying to line up sailing dhows for a sunset shot in a beer commercial. We had to translate from English to Arabic and from Arabic to Swahili using two interpreters. By the time everybody was sailing along together, the sunset was almost over!"

"It's a form of self-therapy."

LARRY K.

It all started with a small car collection—Matchbox cars. "I had a difficult childhood," says Larry. "When I married and settled down and had children, I wanted them to have the toys I never had. One of the things I started to do was on each payday, I would buy a Matchbox car for my son. I think we ended up with about four thousand of them."

But that wasn't the end of Larry's collecting. From Matchboxes he moved up to pedal cars. "When I was a kid I always wanted to have one," he says. "So I started collecting them for my kids. Of course, the kids grew up and moved on, but I never did. I just kept collecting!"

With well over a hundred pedal cars in his collection, crunch time came when Larry and his wife retired to Kentucky. Before the move, Larry's pedal cars were displayed around his business, so now he needed to find a solution to housing them in his new home. He decided to build a brand-new barnlike garage on his property, which serves as a showroom as well as a place to keep his farming equipment.

"Some of the older cars here were giveaway promotional items," Larry explains. "You bought a Cadillac from the dealer and he gave you a pedal car replica, a Kidillac, for the kids." Walking down the lines of cars, he picks out some examples: "There's a '55 Studebaker, a '50 Mercury, and a '39 Pontiac—and they all look exactly like the original cars from that time."

He adds, "It was the same with tractors. They were more than just toys—they were a way to get the customer to buy a John Deere, a Ford, or an Oliver tractor."

"The heyday of the pedal car was over by the '60s," explains Larry. "By then the practice of copying an existing car was considered a patent infringement. After that, the pedal cars they produced didn't resemble anything real and the charm was lost."

Larry is "trying" to be a farmer these days. "I spend most of my time outside planting grapes and blueberries and pulling weeds," he says. "But when the weather's bad, my dog Harley and I come inside to work on the cars."

"The kids outgrew the cars,

but I never did."

THE SUSPECTS

"It's middle-aged men acting like fourteen-year-old boys, but with a hint of maturity . . . sometimes," laughs Stu, lead guitar and vocals, as he describes The Suspects. However much The Suspects joke about their ages, though, they all agree that without the many years of collective knocks, they wouldn't be enjoying the success they're having right now.

"We've all played in many different bands over the years and experienced how very silly problems can break up a group" says Kenny, The Suspects' drummer. "In fact, it's because of a 'gig gone wrong' with a band Rick and I played in—after which I was convinced I was through with drumming forever—that The Suspects was formed."

Tom, second lead guitar and vocals, picks up the story: "I was in the audience the night of that 'blow up.' I had played with Kenny several years earlier, and I had great memories of the old times. I decided to give him a call the next day, just to get reacquainted. Before we knew it, we were talking about starting a new band." And the first person they invited to join them was their mutual friend and lead vocalist, Rick.

Next, The Suspects went looking for bass player. "We were lucky," says Kenny. "Pat here is only twenty-something, and we wondered whether he would want to join a band with a bunch of old farts!" But Pat was curious. "The next question," says Rick, "was would he be interested in playing 'baby boomer' rock music?" So they lent Pat a CD to get acquainted with the sound and were delighted when he still wanted to audition. Tom laughs, "We old guys were thrilled—he certainly helps dial up our ailing sex appeal."

Kenny met Stu when he installed a hot-water heater in Stu's garage. "I was blown away by his guitar collection," Kenny recalls. "And it turns out

he'd been a musician for over thirty years." Last but not least was Max on keyboards. "We posted an ad on the Internet," says Stu, "and the first time he played with us, we knew he was a great fit."

Twice a week the usual Suspects roll into Tom's garage for rehearsal. There's not much room in the soundproof studio he's created there, what with Kenny and his drums jammed into the corner, but the sound is great and the band is popular—booked for the summer. As Stu says, "You're never too old to rock and roll!"

"There are no big egos."

ANDY

"Growing up in America, Harley Davison was the only 'home-grown' motorcycle. To me, it's the ultimate machine," says Andy.

Andy's been riding Harleys for thirty-six years, and it's his passion for those machines that has dictated many of the best decisions of his life. For one thing, he is happily married to a "Harley Woman"—she rides a Dyna Low Rider, he rides a Road King, and, of course, they spend lots of time riding together. "We've taken some great trips on the Heritage Softail Classic," Andy says. "Up and down the west coast from Mexico to Washington and over to the east coast, through the Appalachians, and down to Key West."

Andy points out another Harley-based decision that worked out well. "When we were looking for the site for our new home," he says, "we knew we wanted enough room for a house and a big garage"—and they found it! The nine-car garage ended up being six hundred square feet larger than their house, which they both agree makes sense.

This is what Andy's all about. He likes having a place to relax and party with friends after a day out riding with the local Temecular Valley HOG chapter. His garage more than fits the bill: there's ample room to accommodate more than a hundred Harleys on the enormous forecourt and, as if that weren't enough, the garage sits on a hilltop with a quarter-mile driveway that snakes up from the road below. "You should hear the sound of a hundred Harleys coming up that driveway," says Andy. "Music to my ears!"

"But my six grandkids are the ones who really terrorize the driveway," Andy laughs. Naturally, they all have their own little bikes, and he's made sure the garage has plenty in it to amuse them: there's a train set that runs on a track above the pool table, a foosball table, and an intercom to "order in" sandwiches from the house.

For Andy and his fellow riders, the Harley experience continues long after they dismount their bikes. In addition to the well-stocked garage bar, the pool table, and the card table, there's a Harley jukebox, a Harley pinball machine, and—you guessed it—even a Harley-themed bathroom!

Yes, Andy's got a lot to thank his Harleys for.

"It's a passion. People either love them or hate them."

TOMMY

"I had just moved from California to Florida. I was driving around, feeling a bit out of place, when I saw all these families out boating on the bay," says Tommy. "I immediately knew, 'That's it! I need a boat!' So I turned the car around and went and bought my Hewes flats boat." After that, things fell right into place for Tommy: he found a house with a garage big enough to store his new boat—and it even

bordered a wildlife preserve with a generous natural pond. A few bass and bluegills tossed into the pond, and Tommy had a fly fisherman's dream house!

A musician and composer by trade, Tommy juggles a hectic work schedule and parenting his two young children. Needless to say,

finding himself a bit of quiet time now and then is a real treat. "Some days, if I'm organized, I drop the kids off at school, then drop the boat in the water and head out," he says. "I like to cut the engine and pole the boat quietly through the shallows—it's very peaceful. If I'm lucky, I catch and release redfish. Then I head back just in time to pick up the kids."

Tommy's job involves quite a bit of travel, which has given him the opportunity to fly-fish the world over. "I've gone fly-fishing in every U.S. state," he says, "as well as great places in the rest of the world—New Zealand, Japan, Chile, Brazil."

Tommy has already lived many of his dreams, but if there's one dream he still holds, it's giving his five closest buddies the fly-fishing trip of a lifetime. The fantasy goes like this: "I win the lottery and I call them up. I say, 'Take three weeks off work and bring nothing but your fishing gear and your wife or girlfriend.' We would start in the Florida Keys and catch bonefish, then drive to the Gulf and fish the 10,000 Islands for snook and redfish. After that, we fly to New Zealand—first class all the way, of course—and there we fish the South Island for brown trout at Rota Rora. Not finished yet, it's on to Alaska for grayling and freshwater rainbow trout before we check out Silver Creek, Idaho, for the very educated and hard-to-catch trout there. We end up in the upper Northeast catching stripers."

He sighs at the thought of someday enjoying that shared fly-fishing experience. "It would be so cool," he says, "and the girls would love it, too!"

"The boat came first, then the house."

DEAN

It may be only a few short steps from his Hollywood Hills home to his garage recording studio, but for Dean it's a world away mentally. "When I'm in it, I know why I'm here," he says. "It's my work space." And work is music; writing it, recording it, and playing it live. It's no surprise, then, to find out Dean was a founding member of the funky 1980s rock band The Motels, or that he later formed his own band, Code Blue.

Dean remodeled his 1929 one-car garage and turned it into a music studio back in the 1990s. At the time he planned to rehearse and record there, since he'd just closed his music studio in Hollywood. "But then an opportunity came along," says Dean, "to manage a Web site dedicated to punk music, as well as to produce and direct punk music videos and Web documentaries." So he decided to take a break from music to move into film and photography. "Twelve years later it was time to move on again," he continues, "and when I finally picked up my guitar again, it was nice to have my old garage studio sitting there waiting for me."

Converting his garage involved adding a couple of small, high windows to the permanently sealed wooden garage door and thoroughly soundproofing the place "so I wouldn't disturb the neighbors." The conversion also included hiding some stubborn concrete-floor oil stains under a carpet. It took him a while to discover one of its quirkier features. "After a long day of sitting in my wheeled chair, I would always wind up pressed against my desk. When I took a level to the garage floor, I found out it has quite a slope to it!" he laughs. "Mystery solved." But the sloped floor is good for recording—it reduces unwanted sound reflections—so he has decided to leave it that way.

Dean's space has nurtured his creativity. "I can concentrate out here and compose without interruption. But at a certain point I need to get out of the garage and take the music on the road to get the audience's reaction." He smiles. "That's what I love most—playing live."

"I'm focused in my garage."

ROB

There are few sounds as chilling as that of a chain saw in a forest—a tree going down, the end of its beauty and its life. But when Rob's chain saw rings out over a wooded canyon high above the California coast, it's the sound of good things happening. That's because he's working wood that he has salvaged from the "urban forest" of his local town. Rob collects wood that would otherwise have ended up being chipped at the local dump or burned in fireplaces. "A terrible waste," he says.

It takes physical effort, resourcefulness, and plenty of storage space to manage these often-giant salvaged trees. With ingenuity and skill, Rob's labors eventually turn gnarly trunks into dried planks and finally into precision-molded floorboards that can be slotted together to form rich mixed-species wooden flooring, one of his specialties. To help him perform his magic, Rob has built the ideal garage work space—large enough to pull his trucks into for rainy-season work and at the same time open and airy enough to allow him to enjoy the area's temperate year-round weather.

Rob's unique garage/workshop is framed with salvaged construction steel so the trailer, which acts as his office, can sit on top of the roof. A fringelike fence fashioned from local bamboo screens the trailer up above and gives a "castaway, Pacific island" feel to the massive structure. On the cement floor below sit workbenches, woodworking tools, lathes, and the compact sawmill that turns out Rob's custom molding.

And there's one more piece Rob considers essential working equipment—his old upright piano. "It took me a long time to find the right piano for my work space," he says. "It had to have just the right feel." As he sits down at the piano, he adds, "This one I found in the desert, and when I opened it up, it smelled of dry air and dust and it was right." With that, Rob's hands fly over the keys and the notes drift off into the trees.

"I'd like to salvage all the local wood."

GEORGE N.

George came of age about the time sci-fi hit the small screen. The "UFOs" took hold of him back then and have never let him go. "I watched all those science fiction movies and television shows in the '60s and '70s," he explains. "That's when I started my collection—I must have at least two thousand old sci-fi magazines from the '60s." Luckily, he has plenty of space in his garage to accommodate such a collection.

His two-car garage was built back in the 1930s in an architectural style that complements the house, a classic suburban Los Angeles Spanish bungalow. But it's the garage's two entrances that really come in handy for George's family: one half functions as a storeroom for the family's odds and ends, while the other half has been completely taken over by George and his hobbies, including his magazine collection.

"My other hobby is model building—especially airplanes," says George. "Models were the big thing when I was growing up. Everyone got them for birthdays and Christmas because in those days they were only 98 cents a pop." Interestingly, he continues, "Those same model kits have become very high end, and they now cost 98 dollars. Of course, with the aftermarket add-ons, like decals and other great 'stuff,' they can even go as high as 200 dollars!" He laughs, "We're the same guys building the same models as when we were kids—it's just that now we have more money to spend on them."

Although George now has more disposable income than when he was a boy, having a garage seems to bring out both his thrifty and his innovative sides. And both those instincts came up winners when he went looking for a model airbrushing station. "One day it just dawned on me that the old fridge in my garage would make a great spray booth. So I removed the door and took a sledgehammer to the freezer section. I cut a hole in the side, made a vent to the outside, and attached a fan. Now it's safe to use my paint and airbrushes."

When he's between shows (George works in television—no surprise!), he has the time to go out to the garage and just hang out. Sometimes he works on one or the other of his hobbies. And sometimes he just enjoys sitting and reading his sci-fi magazines, "traveling through another dimension, a dimension not only of sight and sound, but of mind . . ."

"Watch the skies!"

PAUL G.

"I have this unnatural attraction to European classics," says Paul. "Some may call them junk, but to me they're the orphans I find lost and forlorn on this foreign shore." And, as he explains, "If the 'acquisition terms' are right, meaning free—money-wise," they often end up in his garage.

The 1960 Skoda Felicia up on the rack is a classic Paul acquisition story. It met the criteria—made in the Czech Republic, Paul's father's native land, and it belonged to a little old lady who was looking to give it away. Never one to take advantage, Paul put in a hard day of yard work in exchange for his new 'orphan.' "Now it's in good company," he says "with my Czech Tatra."

That "good company" also includes a crowd of ancient bikes that Paul has rescued from oblivion. Though most of them are desperately in need of parts, mere shells of what they once were, they are destined to one day be returned to their former glory.

Sourcing those much-needed parts is something Paul excels at. Take for example his AJS 1932 British bike. "When I got it, it cried out for a sidecar," says Paul. "One day I spotted what I thought might be a good match, a sidecar made in the 1960s. Would you believe it? That sidecar turned out to be a replica of a 1930s sidecar. When I finally found all the information, it turned out to be nearly identical to the one the bike originally had!"

Paul feels lucky to have found his current garage/workshop space. It fits his needs and his personality perfectly—and he likes that it has an interesting history all its own: "It was built back in the early 1920s on a former movie studio lot," says Paul, "and many of the Keystone Cops movies were filmed around here." Outside, Paul points upward, behind the garage. "The 'cops' used to race up and down that hill right there."

Surrounded by suburbs now, the building has managed to survive—so far. But with each successive owner it has slipped further away from its glamorous heyday: it's been a Piggly Wiggly, an auto parts store, a newspaper warehouse, abandoned, filled with junk, abandoned once again, and finally completely abandoned, only to be rescued and restored by Paul. "I've replastered the walls and repaired the ceiling," he says. "But it may not be long before it's torn down for redevelopment."

When that day comes Paul will have to find another home for his eclectic mix of bikes and cars. But until then he's happy to repair, restore, tinker, create and, yes, acquire more orphans.

"I've rescued a lot of orphans."

BILL H.

"I started building out of my shop when I was a kid because I got tired of borrowing things," says Bill. "And now, some forty years later, I still have the first wrench set I ever bought—I was ten years old and I got it for $26." Bill pulls open the drawer of his megasized red tool chest, in a garage packed with equipment and so large it could pass for an airplane hangar, and places his hand on those very same childhood tools.

And, like his tool collection, Bill's garage—or collection of garages—also had humble origins. "I built everything you see on this lot from scratch," Bill says. Indeed, what many years ago was a Florida orange orchard now hosts a magnificent two-story, antebellum-style house with a pool and several garages that range in size from small to hangar-worthy—with plenty of space to spare. "It all started with this small concrete slab I poured maybe thirty years ago," he explains as he walks a few paces across the yard to the original structure. "I built a shelter over it to keep the sun off my equipment, and from there I built the house, the pool, the shop—everything."

But Bill's real pride and joy is the collection of hot rods that sits in a garage just off his main workshop. "I originally built this room for our kids, but now that they've grown out of it, I've turned it into a hot rod room for me." His collection includes a lipstick red 1934 two-door Tudor sedan, a lavender-colored 1937 Chevy pickup, and a black 1937 Ford Club. And in the corner sits a three-carburetor flathead motor from a '49 Mercury that's destined for new life inside the '37 Ford. "It's nostalgia," according to Bill. "In the last ten years there's been a real comeback in these motors. My wife says we always revert back, and she's right. The sound of these great old motors sure brings back the good old days for me."

"I buy the cars," Bill explains, "but my wife's the one who drives them." To illustrate, he points to the license plate on the lipstick red Tudor that reads "ITS 4 HER." When his wife fell in love with it at a car show, Bill was inspired to make it a surprise gift.

Bill gazes over his great expanse and laughs, "When I was a kid, all I wanted was more and more tools. Now I have all this, with every kind of lathe and milling machine and sandblaster. I think I'm finally getting there!"

"I'm always building something."

DON

Don is clearly a man dispossessed of a garage and any manly space he can call his own.

"I can still remember the days when my Datsun 280 ZX easily fit into the garage, but those times are long gone," he says sadly.

Over the years, as Don's family grew, the house seemed to shrink and the household overload had no place to go but out to the garage—to be

stored, forgotten, and finally abandoned. So now Don's beloved space has become an emotionally sticky sanctuary for plain old household junk, the sentimental keepsakes of three now-grown children, family memorabilia, and materials for his wife's many hobbies. "It's hard for me to even find a space for my tool box," Don laments.

"I hoped that when the kids left home they would take their things as well," says Don. Didn't happen. So, desperate to have his space

back, Don uncharacteristically resorted to making various threats. He even issued deadlines, after which he threatened to take matters into his own hands and chuck out all the junk. His "scare tactics" fell on deaf ears. One memorably misguided effort to get a daughter's attention ended in tragedy when Don defiantly hauled her Raggedy Ann doll outside and placed it next to the trash bin. "Unfortunately," he sadly recounts, "the garbage collectors came earlier than usual that day and," he sighs, "I've still not been forgiven."

"I've actually given up any hope of getting this cleared out now," says Don as he heaves open the garage door to squeeze in several bags of paper towel rolls with his foot. "My neighbor has just built himself a nice shed in his backyard," he continues, with a happier look on his face. "I'm thinking of building one just for myself and putting a padlock on the door!"

"The last time I had a car in my garage was in 1976."

ERIC

When Eric found a very large garage attached to a modest apartment, he knew he'd found the right place. The previous occupant had extended the garage out to nearly triple its original size—just what Eric needed. You see, he is an artist, and his medium is colored Plexiglas. It's a material he is very much at home with, having grown up surrounded and inspired by the work of his father. "Ever since I was a kid," he explains, "I've been exposed to plastic because of my dad, who was a plastic sculpture pioneer in the '60s."

Eric continues, "I like to work with my hands as well as my head." And because his creative process requires the use of several specialized tools he makes himself, he says he gets "the best of both worlds." His paintings begin life at his composing table, where the hundreds of Plexiglas squares that make up his color palette are individually layered in color sequences. As he arranges the colors, the composition of the painting slowly evolves. "Composing the colors is a very relaxing and satisfying process for me," he says. "It draws me into a very captivated zone."

Once the composition portion is completed, Eric re-creates the color sequence using larger squares of Plexiglas, which are stacked and glued together. The resulting block is then cut into hundreds of slices, each containing the original composition. These complex pieces are then laid out flat and juxtaposed to form the final pattern. Once everything is glued together to form a panel, he transfers the painting to the wet-sander/polisher he designed and built himself. This second stage of the design process is, according to Eric, "just plain old processing—rote, mechanical, and tedious." He uses earplugs to cut down on the noise, and his hands become a blur as he maneuvers the sander up and down the length of his current piece, Patchwork.

The results of all this hard grunt work are breathtakingly luminescent kaleidoscopes of color that light up his whole garage—not to mention art galleries and private collections throughout the country.

"I let process bring elements of chance and complexity into the work. . .

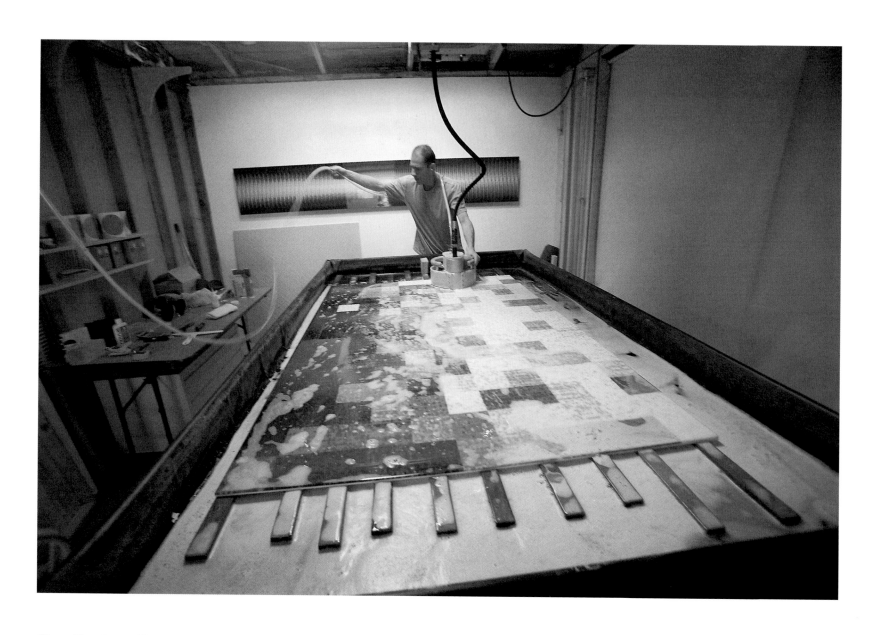

I think this opens a channel of nature."

GEORGE W.

There's a reason George is smiling so broadly: he's a man with a dream who never gave up on it, even when it took four decades to come true. "I thought I had it years ago," he explains, "but just a week after I drove my brand-new dragster race car for the very first time, I was rear-ended on the freeway!" It was a serious accident that, needless to say, blew his dream way off track. "My recovery put me out of work for six months," George continues. "And with a wife and kids to support, the only way we could get by and keep the house was for me to sell the dragster. So that's what I did."

Later, George started his own business, which he ran successfully for more than thirty years. When he finally sold the business and retired, the never-forgotten dream was quick to reclaim its place at the head of the pack: "At last I'm able to get back to drag racing!" And after such a long wait, George is wasting no time. Though he's "still in the testing and tuning phase," he grins with delight when he says, "I have driven the dragster once—and it's really fast!" Then he gets down to nuts and bolts: "It used to be a junior fuel car and runs on alcohol. It's capable of quarter-mile times in the low seven seconds and can reach speeds of 185 miles an hour." George's three best buddies act as his pit crew. "We all have our assigned jobs," he says, "but I'm the driver!"

Selling his business also meant that George was in a financial position to build his dream garage—one that occupies the entire first floor of his new house. "You can drive in one end and out the other—and there are no posts!" The showroom-like garage holds up to seventeen vehicles and is home to all the cars and motorcycles that have significance in George's life: a 1957 Lincoln Continental Mark II, a Ford pickup, a GT 5S Pantera, and a Dodge Viper.

"I'm so fortunate—I never thought I'd be in a position like this in my life," says George, adding with a smile, "Of course, it helps that I have an understanding wife who lets me do whatever the hell I want."

"A lust-filled dream of forty years!"

PAUL C.

It takes Paul less than five minutes to turn the regular workbench in his two-car garage into a space befitting a natural history museum. All he has to do is unpack a few boxes and the work surface disappears under an avalanche of exquisite Native American artifacts.

Although Paul isn't Native American, he has made it his life's work to understand how the early inhabitants of the western United States lived and prospered in what we would call a wilderness. And he is not just a leading academic on the subject—he also practices the skills that the American Indians depended on for their very survival. "Almost nobody today can make fire with the hand drill," Paul explains, "and

Paul says, "I have been able to pass on these skills to a new generation of Native Indians who never had a chance to learn from their elders," you know he knows what he is talking about.

How does a man like Paul reconcile the modern world with the successful, sustainable ways of our forebears? He says one way is to "not forget the lessons of the past," which is the reason he's determined to pass on his knowledge. And, if there's a place on earth where the past and present "almost" collide, it must be right there in Paul's garage when he backs his Toyota Land Cruiser up to within inches of his boxes of Indian artifacts. Luckily, he knows what he is doing.

"I teach skills that have largely been lost."

yet the ability to make fire in the wild is perhaps the most important survival skill a person can possess."

Paul has honed his skills the hard way—through years spent in the wilderness staking his own survival on his ability to reproduce the personal implements and hunting tools of California Natives. Just read a few of the chapter headings from his book on survival and you see how well he knows his subject, like "The Fire Drill," which Paul describes this way: "There is no machine on earth so potent, yet so simple and elegant, as the two sticks of the Native American fire drill." Other chapters deal with such subjects as "Yucca and Agave Fiber Sandals" and "How to Stalk, Kill and Eat a White Throated Wood Rat." And, because Paul is a handyman with both the bow and arrow and the rabbit stick, a boomerang-like device used to fell, yes, rabbits, there is a lot to choose from off the survival menu. And when

LARRY B.

"First I knock off the stone's rough outside," says Larry, "and then the rock starts to speak to me." He knows it may sound crazy to some, but it's the way his sculpting process begins.

A large and empty space is another important part of Larry's work method. "I need room to move around, climb upstairs to view a piece, work on multiple projects at the same time, all the time maintaining my concentration," he says. "And even while I'm in constant motion, I must be able to keep eye contact with the sculpture. If I have to look around to avoid tripping over something it breaks my concentration. Which is the reason," he says, "that I try to keep the garage bits in the garage section and the art in the art section."

Larry's garage sits on a high piece of ground above the Ohio River, amid ninety-five acres of the Indiana State Classified Forest that Larry manages as part of a stewardship program that ensures there will be hardwood timber for future generations.

The massive garage doors make it easy for him to get his forestry equipment in and out and when the doors are open they provide lots of

"I don't like being cramped."

natural light and easy access to his studio. "I was commissioned to do a millennium sculpture for the town of Corydon—a bass relief carved out of a three-ton block of limestone," he says. "For that piece I needed to get a crane right into my space."

"Today I'm working on a sculpture of our dog Frankie," he explains. "She loved me and my wife, and she stuck to us like a cocklebur. But she also loved to chase deer and whatever else got in her way. One day, about a year ago, she was chasing something through the woods, I'm pretty sure it was a deer, and she was hit by a car. Frankie was a small dog," continues Larry, "but she had a big attitude and an even bigger heart. So I carved her out of Colorado alabaster and gave her a deer mask."

"My goal in my art," says Larry "is to produce things of beauty and grace that will be loved and appreciated for a long time. Sculpture is enduring, and when I've passed from this existence it will still be around, I hope, to inspire others to live creatively."

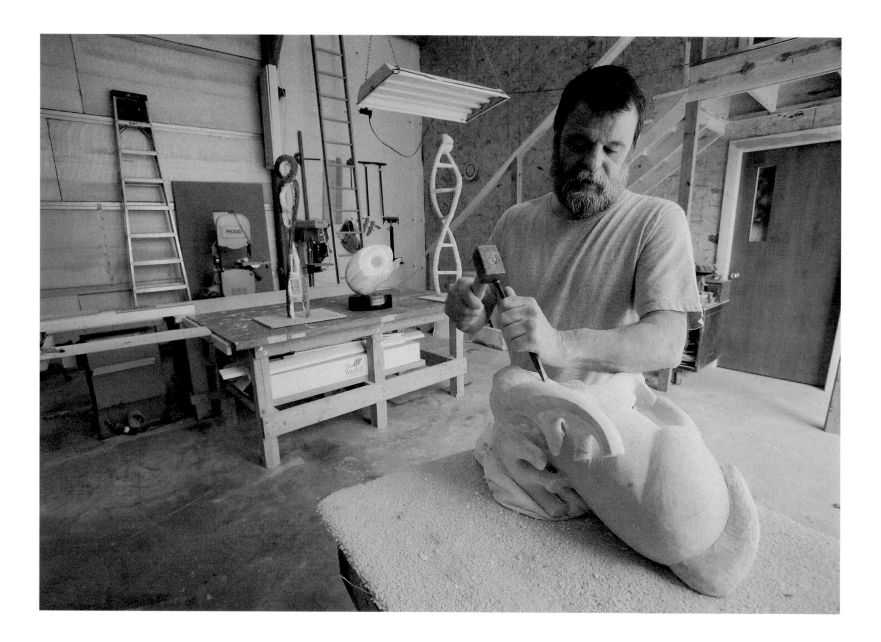

DANIEL

"There are no rules in a garage space," says Daniel. "It allows for ambiguity. You get to decide how things are ordered in your own space, to organize your work areas the way you want." And, he adds, "It's a celebration of a primitive freedom. In public spaces you have to behave in a certain way, but back in your own garage, everything's OK."

If anyone understands the concept of personal space, it's Daniel. He's passionate about it because he believes having a personal space fosters creativity, self-awareness, and, ultimately, fulfillment. "My grandfather was my inspiration and my mentor," he says. "He worked off a small table. My father, on the other hand, had our entire basement for his woodworking shop, but it was entirely off limits to me. It was not a welcoming environment."

Years later Daniel found himself married and living in the city—but he still wanted to explore woodworking, so he put his grandfather's lessons into practice. "I started with a tiny corner in our bedroom in a Manhattan apartment. My wife was very understanding!" he says. "It soon became necessary to move our bed into the living room so I could use the entire bedroom space, though. And when I found I needed still more room, I went looking for shared space in the city, which I found."

Over the years Daniel's woodworking business prospered, and he and his family were able to move to upstate New York. Eventually he came to possess the ultimate "man space"—a nineteenth-century carriage house. "There are certain barriers to people easily entering this space: there's no sign, there's a muddy pathway, then the door around the side, and finally this dusty curtain," he laughs.

These days Daniel helps others succeed. "I've made so much furniture, there's nothing more I really want to make. I really enjoy teaching other people how to make things and explore their creative

sides. Maybe it's just turning sixty. But personally, I'm now busy making hundreds of carvings from pieces of bark I collect from the Hudson River. So I'm not done making, just making furniture. I now share my garage with a clan of bark people!"

"My advice to people is this," says Daniel. "Everybody is always making something: dinner, deals, trouble. . . . Just find a private space, gather a few materials and tools, and see what happens. Making is a primal, spiritual activity, way beyond the marketplace."

"It's a man's space; the atmosphere,

the wood floor—it's soothing."

BOB

"I work on German cars during the week and battle Germans on the weekends. It's kind of ironic!" says Bob. Having a Mercedes repair business and five thousand square feet of garage space means Bob has plenty of room for his "out of control" hobby—World War II reenactment.

"My father was in the Army Air Corps in the Second World War," Bob explains. "He died when I was only nine years old, so I didn't have time to get to know him." But Bob found a way. "One day I saw a display of historic airplanes at a local air show and suddenly realized that maybe if I knew more about the American experience in the war, it could help me know my father better."

So Bob has taken it upon himself to learn as much as possible about World War II history to add context—and poignancy—to the few mementos he has. He points out the photos of his father standing in the North African desert and adds, "I also have my dad's discharge papers and some of the letters he wrote home."

As for his own war "experience," out in the wilds on the weekends, fighting the "enemy," Bob's got himself an impressive array of World War II equipment—all the uniforms and some nice extras: an authentic army cot, a mess kit with rations, a foot locker, walkie-talkies, and an officer's portable field desk. One of his very special treasures is a photograph of a real World War II sweetheart: "It's a picture of my mom sixty years ago," says Bob.

His 1942 Ford jeep came courtesy of a friend in his reenactment group. "He got married," explains Bob simply. "I mean, what usually happens next happened—my friend's jeep had to go to make way for more mundane domestic stuff." So, Bob bought the jeep and mounted his thirty-caliber operational Browning machine gun on the back. Now Bob's customers never know what to expect when they walk in his shop—he's been known to unexpectedly let loose a blank or two from the Browning.

"An ex-girlfriend accused me of being a World Ware II fanatic—can you believe that?" Bob sighs. "I told her it's not an obsession, it's a passion." And sometimes being single has its advantages: "I can still afford to indulge myself, and I don't have to justify buying an old army vehicle when I should be buying a refrigerator."

"Come in, World War II."

BILLY

Most days you can find Billy in his garage, crafting long-handled paddles for the emerging sport of stand-up surfing. With the thriftiness and resourcefulness he says he gets from his mother—who raised him by herself during the Great Depression—he constructs his paddle shafts from salvaged lumber reinforced with carbon-fiber thread and the fiberglass blades from a mold of his own design. Anyone who's lucky enough to own paddles made by Billy can be assured they're the best, because when it comes to paddling, Billy is a world expert.

Back in the early 1970s Billy worked as a swim coach at a Los Angeles high school. But his passion was canoeing, and he often arrived in the school parking lot with a canoe strapped to the roof of his car. "That always drew at lot of attention from the kids," says Billy,

"and they were always begging me to let them try it." He agreed, of course, and happily went one further—he formed a racing club to give the kids a competitive edge.

From there the story becomes the stuff of the great American sports movie: green West Coast underdogs challenge in a sport long dominated by the "establishment" East Coast clubs and, against all odds, win the national title—not just once, but ten times! "We were the first [canoeing] club west of the Mississippi ever to do that," Billy says proudly.

Running a racing club on a shoestring, though, meant that Billy's resourcefulness, and his garage, needed to be kicked into high gear. He built the paddles and the canoes, welded boat trailers together, and even silk-screened the club T-shirts himself. "My philosophy is: nobody gets left out because they can't afford it," says Billy. And, as his coaching fame spread, kids from all over the world came to Billy to be trained. "They came from New York, Texas, Iowa, and as far away as Australia and Argentina—my wife and I always found a way to help them stay."

And then the story gets even better: in 1984, when the Olympics came to town, one of Billy's kids won the gold! For a coach, it just doesn't get any better than that. And that's why Billy says he's a very lucky man, "because I have spent most of my life working at what I would gladly have done for free."

Billy's retired from coaching now so life is a little less hectic, a bit less competitive. He's even "downsized" from a two-car to a one-car garage—just big enough to meet the demand for his long-handled paddles. He'll never relinquish his involvement with water sports.

"I've been lucky."

HAROLD

Harold, like four previous generations of his family, is a boatbuilder. Specifically, he builds and repairs Adirondack Guide Boats in the spacious two-story garage that sits next to his home on the sloping hillside of a beautiful Adirondack lakeshore. "And now my grandson is showing an interest in joining the family business!" Harold beams.

Over the years Harold has built seven Adirondack Guide Boats himself using the traditional woods of red spruce for the ribs and beveled and lapped white cedar for the side planking, securing it all with tiny copper nails. But when he says he should have built it longer, he's talking about the workshop above his garage, not about a boat. He wishes his workshop were bigger to better accommodate the large, specific design of these time-honored vessels.

These elegant boats date back to the early 1800s and have a special place in the area's history. As Harold explains, "Local guides in the Adirondacks needed boats that were large enough to carry themselves and the city 'sports' who employed them, plus all the camping and hunting equipment, dogs, and the spoils of the hunt." At the same time, at fifteen to seventeen feet and sixty-five to seventy-five pounds, the craft had to be fast and durable enough to weather the winds and waves of the mountain lakes. "Yet the boat still had to be light enough for the guide to carry across the land between lakes by himself," Harold adds, pointing to the place in the boat were a wooden yoke could be fitted amidships so that the upturned craft could sit squarely on the guide's shoulders.

Back in those days, according to Harold, "there were lots of lakeside boatbuilders and they all had their own unique styles." And, there's one more important feature of these boats: "They built them to last.

Right now I'm repairing a Caleb J. Chase of Newcombe boat that's 150 years old."

Watching Harold work in this peaceful and timeless place, it's hard to imagine him ever doing anything other than plying the family boatbuilding trade. But that couldn't be further from the truth. Harold, or "Hoss," as he was known back in his U.S. Navy pilot days, used to fly high-altitude reconnaissance photography missions, zooming to speeds of Mach 1.5 and reaching altitudes as high as sixty-five thousand feet, refueling his Vaught F8 plane in midair. "We weren't supposed to go that high, but we did it anyway," says Harold with a smile on his face as he remembers an experience few people will have. "You felt like you were going to drop off the edge of the world up there."

"I just wish I had built it forty feet longer."

CLAIR

Clair will be the first to tell you what a good feeling it is to finally realize a cherished dream: "I've spent all my life looking after my family, so it's nice to have reached the point where I can start on some of the projects I've always wanted to do." One of his dreams was to restore a vintage car, and he built a two-car garage so he would have room to do just that.

"I didn't want to create a showpiece, though," Clair says of the car. "I have nine grandchildren, and the little ones love to ride around with me." He found the perfect project in the form of a 1936 Chevrolet. "This car was just right," he says. "The body was in good shape, and I knew the repair work was something I could handle myself."

Clair's '36 Chevy came with its original straight-six engine that included a single-barrel carburetor. The original spare tire was in good shape and so was the heating system, which "still works like a charm." Clair unlatches one side of the hood and reaches into the engine compartment to demonstrate the "on/off" heating switch—a shutoff valve attached to the air intake. "All you had to do back then was drive around long enough for the engine to warm up, stop the car, get out, open the hood, open the shutoff valve, close up the hood, and get back in!"

One unique and nostalgic feature of the '36 Chevy is its wheel and brake cylinders, and Clair has had firsthand experience with this vintage technology. "Back then they had a suspension system called 'knee action suspension' where the cylinders were filled with oil and really provided a good ride through hydraulic action." The problem with this system, according to Clair, was that the oil often leaked out. "My grandfather had a Chevy with empty cylinders and, boy, do I remember what a crashing-hard ride it was!" Maybe that's why

"It's something I've always wanted."

Clair just happens to mention, "I've restored my suspension to a very comfortable ride."

So, with his project now completed, what will Clair do with his spare time? "I wouldn't mind doing some wheeling and dealing," he says. "What I'd really like is a '37 coupe. I saw one on the road the other day, but I couldn't get the guy to agree to a price. If I find the right one, though, I'll trade up and start again."

CHAS

"I'm my own hardware store," says Chas as he surveys his garage metalworking shop. His clients are sculptors, and his expertise is building support frames for their massive and complex pieces of art. "My professional welding pays my way, and I enjoy it. But I have a master's degree in music, and the real magic for me is playing with the instruments."

Metal shop musical instruments? Maybe we should go back to the beginning . . . "My first instrument was the piano. I had instructors and practiced and practiced, but I just didn't have 'it.' Then I was seduced by the pedal steel guitar—a very demanding mistress."

It hadn't escaped Chas's notice, though, while working in his professional capacity with pieces of steel and titanium, that metals have their own unique sound. "I love the sound of titanium," he says. "It's very 'musical' and can produce very complicated sounds. The conventional sound of European music is twelve pitches to an octave. Once you get beyond twelve-tone octaves, things really open up." So, Chas became enamored of the microtonal world. And with a workshop full of scrap metal, along with the ability to weld anything together, he started making his own very original musical instruments.

Often working with scrap from aircraft manufacturers, Chas has used pieces like airplane nozzles to good effect. And his creations are as visually exciting as the sounds they produce; polished and gleaming, they seem almost alien in form. It's no surprise, then, that he's given them appropriate names like "The Scepter," "Mantis," and "DADO."

But Chas's favorite creation is "The Towers"—long titanium rods

capped with flat metal plates that hang suspended from his recording studio ceiling. When he strikes them with wooden mallets, he gets them all shuddering and murmuring in and out of harmonic unity, creating "phrases"—his name for his unique musical scores.

"If I ever have, say, six to eight weeks between welding jobs, I like to compose," says Chas. "That's the ideal situation." Of course, a man with a passion can always find the time. And since his recording studio is an extension of his garage, he can slip back there and play when the mood grabs him. "Late at night, when I'm too tired to think, that's an interesting time to record."

According to Chas, "Retirement is when you give up on your dreams—not when you start them. What am I going to do when I can no longer do this? That's why I'm doing it now!"

"My life is all about metal."

ROGER

Roger's garage is an old iron foundry that he salvaged when it got in the way of the city's road-widening plans. He took it apart piece by piece, hauled it up to his mountain property, and reassembled it. Now the building sits peacefully under wide oaks, with pieces from its productive days—iron wheels, gratings, and boiler plates—scattered amid the grass and scrub oaks. The foundry's cavernous shape, with its high roof and spreading beams, gives Roger plenty of scope for his eclectic and ever-growing collection of "stuff." The foundry garage also provides a practical work space and ample storage for his five motorbikes.

It was back in 1965 when Roger and his wife moved up to these mountains. "We were hippies then," he says, "and were thinking about having babies. We couldn't afford a house in the nice neighborhood where we came from, so we rented three or four cabins up here, raised chickens, and grew stuff organically." When Roger saw ten acres come up for sale, he and his friend Ted scraped together enough cash to buy it. That was almost forty years ago, and neither Roger, nor his wife, nor Ted has left this wild paradise.

Now, as Roger gets older, he spends more and more time in his foundry garage. He maintains that "men like to gather around them the things that please them, and that's why having a space of their own is very important." Roger has a great affinity for objects with

stories behind them. Take, for example, the massive military-looking canvas trunk with a sturdy wicker interior and three initials stenciled on the outside that he found at an estate sale. "This trunk once belonged to a local officer who shipped out to Europe back in World War I," he says. "It looked interesting to me, so I bought it. When I got it home, buried among the old underwear inside I found love letters written to the officer from his wife!"

What do you do with such things, the last link to a life and its passions so long gone? It's a question that saddens Roger, reminding him how easily the past slips away—which is why he hangs on to just a few old things in his garage.

"It's a place for a man to gather things that are unacceptable in the house."

JIM O.

Jim's lifelong love affair with history began when a World War II veteran from the neighborhood offered his old U.S. Army helmet and a German canteen to the curious and imaginative eight-year-old. With such new "toys" to play with, history came alive that day, and though the Second World War had just ended, for one youngster it had only just begun.

It wasn't long before Jim was collecting every bit of war memorabilia he could get his hands on, "stashing most of it in my parents' basement," he says. And as his passion for all things World War II grew, so did his education. According to Jim, "My father owned the local drive-in theater, and I think I saw every war movie ever made!"

But it's not just World War II history that Jim came to love. He grew up and still lives in Indiana's oldest town, Vincennes, and he's taken to preserving not only the town's history, but also, in his own way, the history of an era—the 1940s and '50s. It's no surprise, then, that much of the town's local color, along with Jim's own childhood, has ended up in his very large garage. He has only to walk a few steps across his backyard to dial back half a century and sit at the soda fountain he enjoyed as a boy, or to listen to the jukebox, or hear the National cash register make that old ka-ching sound.

Of course, the war years are well represented in the garage, too. And Jim's father ran a service station in the 1930s, so he's also got one of those in there—gas pumps and all—fully stocked with vintage fan belts, oil, cigarettes, and victory stamps and adorned with an old World War II poster that asks, "Are you playing square?"

An admitted packrat, Jim says, "When you collect an entire era's domestic and military paraphernalia, space can become an issue." He

thought he'd solved the problem by opening the Indiana Military Museum, but he ran out of space there, too—hence the need to build an extra-large garage behind his house. Jim would be quite happy to never see a modern-day car in it, but he had to strike a deal with his wife. "I promised there would always be room for her car in the winter. It's a promise I've kept—but it hasn't been easy," he sighs.

"It was either build a garage or hold an auction!"

SIR GILBERT

"I fix everything myself," says Sir Gilbert. "I've hired only two tradesmen in my life, and I'm sure both of them were very sorry!" The first thing he did when he got his garage was "fix it" because, according to Gilbert, "it wasn't big enough." He pushed the front wall out and created enough space behind the cars to build a workroom. "It's a bit of an odd shape now, but it works!"

So how did Sir Gilbert, a brass foundry general manager in Scotland, end up with a garage to fix in America? It all started back in the 1960s with a vacation to sunny California. "It was the coldest and dreariest of winters in Scotland," he explains, "and just the thought of going back to the rain and gloom depressed the heck out of me." But fate soon stepped in and a life-changing decision was made when Gilbert and his wife happened upon a house for sale. "It took us about six minutes to make up our minds to buy it," he says. Forty years later they still happily call that house—and the garage that came with it—"home."

Gilbert's new life in America really took off when, soon after they bought the house, he was offered a job in the booming space industry. "I was hired as an engineer but spent my life working as a technician—which was much more fun," he says. Among the projects he participated in over the years were solar panel deployment for the Hubble telescope and a magnetometer boom for the Voyager probe.

But his garage is the place where Gilbert really lets his creativity flow. Twenty-five years ago he embraced the then-fledgling sport of hang gliding. When he failed his landing test—mercifully, not a crash but a failure to land on target—he took a hard look at how better instrumentation would improve his flying skills. "Motorless aircraft, keen on staying up, need to know when the air currents are going up or down, and in a hang glider you go up and down fast like a yo-yo," he explains. "The only variometers we had back then worked far too slowly for coastal flying." So, in typical Gilbert fashion, he fixed that problem by inventing, in his garage, "the first electronic altimeter able to read to a single foot, combined with the quickest—even to this day—variometer." And, according to Gilbert, "They sold like hotcakes!"

Gilbert's current garage project is designing a circuit board that will compare air temperature readings between his roof space and living room. When the roof air tests warmer, a fan will be switched on and warm roof air will be pumped into the living room. Garage ingenuity at its best!

"I'm a fixer."

RICHARD

There's a world of nostalgia in Richard's 1962 two-car garage—in the form of cars, surfboards, and motorcycles.

How he acquired the house and garage sounds a bit like serendipity: "My wife and I were unsuccessfully house-hunting when I spotted this new 'For Sale by Owner' listing in the real estate section of the newspaper. It jumped out at me because of the house number, 1954—same year as my car." Richard shakes his head in amazement. "It turned out to be just what we were looking for and, would you believe it, the owners wanted us to have it so badly, they reduced the price!"

The car that inspired Richard's house purchase was a 1954 Ford Ranch Wagon. "The guy who sold it to me said he'd added some stylish taillights from a 1954 Oldsmobile." Richard laughs as he points them out. "He said they look like Carol Doda's pasties!"

Removing the surf board strapped to the Oldsmobile roof, Richard continues, "This surfboard is from the late '50s or early '60s, the days when surfing was all about long boards and empty surf spots up and down the California coast. This board, though, holds some especially great memories for me." He explains, "I bought it from a good surfing buddy when he needed some quick cash. He promptly repaid the debt and took the board back, but soon after that he passed away. Luckily, my buddy's girlfriend, knowing our close history and the history of the board, felt

I should be the one to take care of it. I think my buddy would have liked that."

And because kismet seems to follow him around, building motorcycles, once just Richard's hobby, has turned into quite a profitable enterprise. It all started when his mechanic, a British Triumph motorcycle enthusiast, convinced Richard to purchase the entire lot of spare parts his sales rep was trying to offload. Richard plunked down his money and proceeded to do the only thing he could do with all that stuff—build more British bikes! He is now the happy proprietor of a thriving business building custom bikes for special clients.

A prime example of his work is his 1967 BSA Hornet racing bike. It has a custom fuel tank, handmade side covers, a seat he found on eBay, aluminum wheels, shorty mufflers, and velocity stacks on the carburetor. "BSA stands for Bastard Shakes Apart," he laughs. "No, really it stands for Birmingham Small Arms, the company that once made small arms and motorcycles for the British army. They went out of business in 1974, but they've helped keep me in business ever since!"

"I find solace here."

ROBY

Walk into Roby's garage and you could find yourself nose to snout with a life-size velociraptor, or shaking hands with an extinct hominid, or startled by the horned dragonlike skull of a newly discovered dinosaur species. These are everyday companions, though, for Roby, a designer and sculptor whose business is re-creating extinct and nearly extinct creatures for natural history and science museums.

"My friends and neighbors are used to it," says Roby as he surveys the unusual contents of his garage studio. "For five years we had a thirteen-foot-tall woolly mammoth in the front garden—just testing to see how he would hold up to the outdoors. After five years of hot East Hampton summers, freezing winters, and torrential rain, we

knew he would hold up anywhere in the world." Then he adds with a grin, "It was a lot more fun than having a garden gnome."

Roby took an unusual road to his unusual line of work. First, he trained as a classical sculptor in Italy, after which he obtained a degree at the London International Film School. "The leap from film to museum work wasn't all that difficult," he says. Certainly not difficult for a man who can make the imaginative leap from skull and bones to fully fleshed-out animal.

How does he do it? "I do a lot of intensive research," says Roby. "I talk to experts and get their opinions about the animal's probable lifestyle." And, in the case of the stygimoloch skull, with its odd assortment of spikes, horns, and nodules, he reveals, "After many late nights sculpting its head, I began to 'see' the entire creature pacing back and forth across my studio as if he were waiting impatiently for me to finish!"

But it's not just extinct species that Roby re-creates. He's been involved in many endangered-species projects where the real-life specimens are now so rare that only models can be exhibited. "It's a sad and sobering world I work in," Roby sighs. "I'm either working in the past to re-create long-extinct creatures, or I'm making copies of those who face imminent extinction in the present. It makes me aware of how fragile the environment is."

And what about Bruce, the skull Roby looks at with such genuine affection? "Ah," he says, "I knew him well . . . he was my dog and a very good friend after all."

"Alas, poor Bruce!"

MARK

It's a bird! It's a plane! And if it's in Mark's garage, it's definitely a plane! Twenty years as a U.S. Navy pilot has only fueled Mark's passion for flying. In fact, so great is his love of airplanes, he's recently begun building one of his own.

An aviator's first priority is, of course, safety. Ever mindful of the dire consequences of inferior mechanics, Mark is meticulous in every aspect of the building process. The first step? Erecting the perfect garage for the task.

Built just down the hill from his home so he can always be near his airplane, Mark's garage is spacious, well lit, clean, and organized, with every tool and every instrument in its designated place. In the center of the garage a sheaf of instructions and technical drawings hangs on a wooden easel, and Mark pores over these blueprints as he moves carefully through the construction process.

But it's not as if the design leaves no room for creativity. In fact, Mark's favorite part of building his own airplane is the way the plans allow him to really make it his own. "Some evenings," he muses, "I find it relaxing just to come down here to the garage, sit with the plane, and think." Lately he's been experimenting with the best way to configure the fuel lines. He also adapted the plane's seating to a "side-by-side" configuration because, Mark explains with a smile, "My wife said she didn't want to stare at the back of my head all day. This way, she can ride beside me and enjoy the view."

Mark has always wanted to fly, and when asked to describe his feelings about it, says: "Flying is like looking at the world from your own private hilltop with an ever-changing view. It's freedom and being in control. It's a feeling of exhilaration coupled with moments

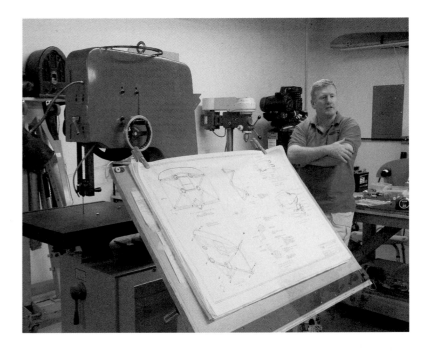

of heart-pounding terror. When flying you need to leave all of life's problems on the ground and focus on the job at hand. Life seems a lot simpler when flying—dangerous at times, but that too can be thrilling."

Once his tests flights are completed, Mark can put his Lycoming engine through its paces, taking the craft as high as fifteen thousand feet and, perhaps, looping the loop on the way up. It's beautiful up there in the sky . . .

"I enjoy working out the details."

DOUG

"You could say I'm a hobby nerd and self-taught sax geek," says Doug, making light of his lifelong pastime and latest hobby. But then he waxes philosophical: "Meriwether Lewis blazed a trail across the USA, but my accomplishments are on a smaller scale and closer to home—frontiers can also be small, personal, and focused."

"I like finding old saxes to rebuild," Doug explains. "Some I keep to play, others I sell. I know it's not a very ambitious goal, but it's for my pleasure and I derive the same satisfaction from it as Captain Lewis might have from finding a new bird species or a river." Commenting on the corner of the family's garage—his space—with its display of memorabilia, workbench, funky old guitars, and gleaming brass saxophones, he observes, "It's the only place in my home where I really feel at home. It's my space within a space."

Doug continues, "I restore saxophones for my own gratification. Because I'm not for hire, I take more care, perhaps better care, than anyone else." He is especially careful to preserve the unique sounds of the older instruments. "Older ones have a huskier, mellower sound," he says, "and the 1950s are where my tastes are. Today's sound is louder and brighter—and more cluttered."

Doug explains some of the many factors that contribute to an instrument's sound: "The style of the horn and mouthpiece make a big difference, so it's better to keep horns and mouthpieces matched in age. And the brass alloys used in the older ones have more heft. The downside is that the key work is clunkier in older horns." Locating replacement parts can be a challenge. "I'm working in a pretty arcane market," he says. "I could never have found this stuff before the Internet came along."

Doug has always enjoyed restoring musical equipment. "I came of

"This is what I do."

age in the era of the electric guitar and high school bands. I still like to rebuild vintage guitars and amps, especially old PA amplifiers. But the guitar market has become so high end now that it's lost a lot of its appeal for me. The good news is that old saxophones are still coming out of people's attics, and one can piddle around with a few hundred dollars and find a fine instrument from the '20s, '30s, or '40s made by master craftsmen," he enthuses.

"I still fix family things, too—like toys, hair clips, and shoes—for my wife and daughters," Doug says. But no surprise here: "I've recently taken on fixing the woodwinds for my kid's school."

ONDRAY

"I live with six women—my wife and our five daughters," Ondray says. As he surveys his neat and compact garage, he explains, "Since I'm the only man in the house, they all understand that I need something that's my very own space." Of course, Ondray is happy to concede part of his garage to family storage needs. And he points with pride to the row of softball bats and helmets that lines one wall: "Three of my girls play softball, and two of them are also into soccer."

But before marriage and family became his number one priority, Ondray met and fell in love with another—his Mustang GT 5.0. After twenty years together, it's clear the man-car love affair is still going strong. "It was the first and only car I ever bought for myself, brand new off the lot," he explains. Yes, there have been other new cars in Ondray's family, "but those belong to my wife."

Ondray's attachment to the Mustang is the reason it gets to live in the garage while the other newer and costlier cars sit outside—and it's probably also why the Mustang, after so many years, still shines with its original paint. But now, as the family car needs have changed, the Mustang has taken on a different role in his life. According to Ondray, "It's become a project car. I'm giving it more personality, and I work on it whenever I can, one thing at a time." So far, he's added a stabilizer bar, underdrive pulleys, a high-performance clutch and shifter, upgraded throttle body and fuel injectors to add flavor to the octane, and an exhaust system by Bassani. Future plans are to replace the upper and lower intake manifolds to add more horsepower.

But the work he enjoys most is detailing the engine parts, most of which are polished or chromed. "I've had the alternator, water pump, smog pump, air conditioner casing, upper and lower manifold, and many other parts either polished or chrome-plated, and the chromed valve covers are waiting to be installed." Ondray explains that chroming can be overdone, though, and says the upkeep is difficult, so he's decided he won't be doing much more of it.

"My car is my baby—and I really enjoy my time with it." So, while Ondray says the Mustang will eventually be a show car, he doesn't appear to be in any hurry to get the job finished.

"This is definitely my space."

COWBOY

It was Cowboy's mother who introduced him to surfing. "She was a beach chick," he says. "When I was only five years old, she put me on her board and paddled me out into the surf." It's almost as if Cowboy's mother birthed him twice: once to the world and again to the waves. "She teases me that she should never have put me on that first surfboard," he laughs, "because I've done nothing else since." And Cowboy confesses that's true. "I always tell people that surfing is a way of life. It's not a sport."

Fifty years ago, when Cowboy entered the waves, surfboards were massive fiberglass-and-resin-coated balsa and redwood long boards. Little Cowboy struggled to drag those heavy boards back into the surf and, not surprisingly, he quickly wore the "tails" off them. But the youngster soon learned how to patch his boards. "Back then you did your own repairs with resin and volan glass from a marine yard," Cowboy recalls, "and I got fast and good at 'ding' repair." So good that before long, he was a "dinger" for all his high school buddies' boards, too. "I'll always be a dinger," he says, as he reaches for the electric hand sander his parents bought him more than forty years ago.

By the mid-1960s, the short board revolution was gathering momentum and long boards were on their way out. Surfboard manufacturers, however, with a huge inventory of long boards to move, were reluctant to change. Cowboy wasn't. He seized the opportunity to stay ahead of the curve and began making some of the first short boards out of existing long boards. "I stripped off the glass resin and cut them down to fit a template that I still use today," he says. He rapidly went from "dinger" to "garage shaper," and while still in high school, found he had a thriving business going.

Cowboy has lived long enough to see a renewed appreciation of

long boards, and he now finds he's one of the few garage shapers still around with the knowledge and skill to restore them. His services are always in demand, not only for the restoration of old long boards, but also for building new custom short boards. It's a situation he is happy to find himself in.

Through all the changes in design and technology, Cowboy has kept his fingers in resin. "Everywhere I've lived there's been resin on the garage floor," he says proudly. "We garage shapers are a dying breed—but it's what I've always done." It seems the waves have shaped not only Cowboy's boards but also his life.

"Garage shapers are still alive, and I'm one of them."

BRIAN

If there is one thing that irritates Brian, it's seeing things thrown away that might come in handy one day. He builds just about everything he needs from salvaged materials that he stores in his garage. Luckily, Brian has a very spacious garage! It didn't start out that way, though. "The first thing I did when I inherited this property was to enlarge the garage," he explains, "because I had to have a big enough space to work in to make all the things I needed to remodel the house."

Brian's home is the house he grew up in—the house his grandfather built in 1925. The original house was a modest, single-story affair but, with the help of a big garage to work from, Brian added a second story himself. He also did all the woodworking, built all the interior cabinetry, and even created the stained-glass artwork that adorns the windows.

No construction task is too big or too small for Brian. When his wife mentioned she would like a nice shoe rack, he rose to the challenge. He disappeared—off to "you know where"—and returned a couple of hours later with the finished item. If the word handyman applies to anyone, it's Brian.

A look around Brian's garage reveals a very active man with many interests. Deer antlers—souvenirs of hunting trips—hang on the walls, sails await repair, a collection of surfboards sits propped in a corner, and a large fishing boat takes up any spare parking space. Every inch of the garage is put to good use storing materials and equipment: scraps of lumber; plastic piping; lots of little plastic drawers with well-sorted widgets, screws, and nails; and all manner of electrical, mechanical, and building tools such as saw horses, a table saw, and a heavy-duty sail-maker sewing machine.

Happily for Brian, his love of building and fixing things goes hand in hand with his occupation: managing apartment buildings that are in constant need of upkeep and repair. Whether it's a cupboard handle needed here, a coat of paint there, or a loose tile somewhere else, Brian's the guy with the resources to fix it—right here in his garage.

"Everything I need is in the garage."

JIM W.

As you enter his massive garage, you pass a framed photograph of Jim at age fifteen, smiling from the hood of a 1950s Ford pickup truck. "That truck was like a first love," he says. But, like so many other young romances, a boy's wild ways spelled doom for the relationship.

The problem was speed. "I just could never resist putting my foot to the floor," Jim laughs. "So by the time I was eighteen, I owned four cars and thirty-nine speeding tickets!" He also remembers what a good run he had at it before the long arm of the law caught up with him. "I sped through just about every city and town," Jim explains, "but since it all happened in the days before everything was linked by computer, it took the police a while to connect me with all those

tickets." When the authorities finally caught up with him, everything hit the fan. They took away his driver's license, and his auto insurance went through the roof—as did his mother. "She made me get rid of all my cars, including my Ford pickup."

But Jim never forgot that old truck. He became so obsessed with

"It's all memory stuff."

getting it back that he even began having nightmares about it. "I would dream that my uncle had it stored safely in his garage, then I'd wake up with a start to find it gone!" As the years went by, he found himself thinking over and over again, "If only I'd been able to keep it!" Jim says it's a longing many men have. "I meet them all the time at car shows, and they all say the same thing: they wish they still had their first car."

Luckily for Jim, he found a cure for his malady. "I tell other guys they owe it to themselves to go find that car and buy it. And if they don't have the money, build it!" That's exactly what Jim did, but in his case it wasn't just one car—he's amassed an entire collection of great memories. He has a Model T C-Cab in honor of the one he built with his father way back when, and then there's the 1941 Seagrave fire truck he bought for his wife before she died "because she always wanted a red truck." And, of course, there's the old Ford pickup—not the original, but close enough to make the nightmares stop. It's no surprise, then, that the sign hanging above the entrance to Jim's garage reads "Memory Lane."

TED

It all started when Ted took a trip back to his native Poland and saw a picture of a Polish World War II tank on the cover of a magazine. "Suddenly I was about nine years old again, playing in view of those tanks. I even remember how they smelled of diesel smoke," Ted recalls. Then he makes a surprising comment: "That picture brought back some of the happiest memories of my childhood." As if feeling the need to explain, he adds, "My father was the managing director of a military vehicle factory and, with the war coming, Poland was gearing up fast to meet the expected German invasion. That tank factory was my childhood playground."

In September 1939 the Nazis did invade Poland, and the Second World War began. Young Ted, however, saw the events of those days through eyes not yet touched by the horrors of war. "To me, the good news was I likely wouldn't have to start school that year!"

Years later Ted became an electrical engineer and founded a successful engineering business from which he is now retired. But while retirement offered him the chance to enjoy painting and other hobbies, Ted the engineer still felt the need to build something. So, since his three-car garage was already filled with three cars, he just added an extension to it—a well-equipped room, more like a laboratory than a garage—and began his work.

It took Ted three years to build his tank. "I started by measuring precisely every detail in this photograph," he explains, holding up the Polish magazine cover, "and then looked for the materials to build it. I used sheet stainless steel from an old oven fume hood. Then I found some local scrap cold-rolled steel to use for the armor plates—it was perfect. And the big wheels on either side are machined from large hardware washers bought

at Home Depot." Ted built the entire tank from the ground up, mostly from scrap metal, even down to the rivets that hold the tank together. And he's even added miniature tool chests complete with tools and a supply of artillery shells that can be loaded into the main gun.

"It all works," says Ted as he sets the tank on the floor and sends it buzzing around with a remote control, stopping now and then to swing the gun turret onto some imaginary target. Gun? "Oh, everyone asks about the gun," he laughs. "The gun's the only part that doesn't work."

"I know those tanks—

and I can build one!"

CHARLIE

Charlie collects! "One week it's lanterns, the next it's jam jars. I just keep going and going to the point where I think it's a sickness," he says. "I need to see a doctor maybe, because I don't even have garage space for my truck anymore." As he backs his flatbed into the carport and starts shoveling items off to one side—spoils from his latest collecting trip—he adds, "Every time I fill up a barn, I have to park my truck in the next one. And now all five barns are full!"

Charlie's collections run the gamut of mundane domestic and industrial stuff. From cast-iron cooking pots to high-voltage insulators; from books, coffee mugs, and tea kettles to farm tools, animal cages, and vacuum cleaners—the list is as endless as the precarious and tottering heaps of stuff are high.

But there are also many unusual items that might well have been lost forever had Charlie not saved them from further decay. He particularly likes the dual-compartment V-shaped tobacco setter for planting tobacco by hand—a local tool that Charlie says would have been a common sight around his Kentucky home a hundred years ago. Walk a little farther and he points out an intriguing handmade wooden horse-drawn seed-sowing device that he believes may be one of a kind.

If there is one recurring theme that marks Charlie as a true collector, it's the sheer number of similar items he keeps. "I reckon I have at least three thousand fishing poles, twenty thousand farm implements, and over two thousand pieces of cast iron," he confides.

To the casual observer, it may defy belief that with five barns full to the rafters, Charlie can possibly keep track of his vast collection, but then, you just don't know Charlie. "I noticed a fishing reel missing the other day. Turns out my daughter took it—but I'll want it back!" And once in a while his wife likes to sneak an item into his collection, just for fun. But Charlie's always quick to spot any additions that haven't met his seal of approval. "I know a fake immediately," he says.

So now that the flatbed is unloaded, Charlie's turning the ignition key of his Corolla. "Gotta go—auction's at five!"

"It all started when I gave up drinking and smoking."

ROBERT

Robert finally has the nice, big, two-story garage he's always wanted, with room to park three cars comfortably. So how, then, did his perfect garage end up a nightclub?

"It all started with the hot tub," he says. "My friends and I were tired after a day of moving stuff into my new house, so we decided to park it in the garage for the night and break out a few beers." When Robert's impending birthday came up in the conversation, it didn't take long before the hot tub sitting in the middle of the garage inspired thoughts of a luau-themed party. "Suddenly my friends swung into action," continues Robert. "They built a bar in the corner, rolled in Astroturf, hung a disco ball from the ceiling, and piped in some great music." What ensued was, according to everyone in attendance, "the party of a lifetime." Tiki Rob's was born!

Though Tiki Rob's was never meant to be permanent, the parties continued long after Robert's birthday had passed. "Everybody preferred partying at Tiki Rob's to going downtown on weekends," Robert explains. "And since my fiancée and I love throwing parties, I wasn't unhappy with the idea of keeping it."

Once the decision was made, Robert threw his heart into making Tiki Rob's a truly knockout experience. He added a video projector with an eight-foot-wide drop-down screen and installed an even better sound system. But he wasn't done yet—more disco lights were definitely called for, not to mention a dance floor, and what's a club without a stripper pole and a poker table? Almost finished, he needed just one more thing to make it perfect—a smoke machine to set the mood! "It's not just a nightclub," Robert says. "Tiki Rob's is its own world."

Robert opens his kitchen back door and steps over the threshold into Tiki Rob's. He pauses on the first-floor landing to take in the consummate nightclub scene below: disco music thumping, colored lights swirling through the fog, steam rising from the hot tub, and a cozy bar in the corner. He pushes a button and the garage door rattles its way up. The smoke clears into the night, and a driveway and a Lexus come into view. The chill Seattle wind blows autumn leaves in across the Astroturf floor, and suddenly the spell is broken . . . it is just a garage after all.

"It's my adult playroom."

GARY

Gary is a man who stays attached to his roots—a charming hamlet in rural upstate New York. He even makes his home in the maternity hospital where he was born, converted many years ago into a house. And within spitting distance stands the stately two-story wooden structure where Gary and his father once ran the family garage business.

The building came to life well over a century ago as a blacksmith shop. For years the business thrived as the town's center for horse-shoeing and wagon repair, but by the 1930s the world had moved on and the blacksmith had gone the way of the horse and buggy. Gary's father took over the shop in 1932 and transformed the building into a garage to meet the demands of the changing times. When Gary finished school, he happily joined his father in the business. As he says, "We mechanics were the new blacksmiths."

So the old blacksmith shop, now a garage, continued to play a vital role in the small community. For many years Gary and his father serviced the area's equipment and vehicles, repairing everything from farm and snow plows, to lawn mowers and tractors, to fire trucks and, of course, most of the town's automobiles. But then came the mid-1980s and all the modern cars were run by computers, backed by 50,000-mile warranties. Progress had taken the tinkering heart and soul out of his business, so Gary closed up his shop. He never sold the building, though, and to this day he is happiest tinkering around his old garage, wrench in hand, repairing the occasional truck and providing bushwhacking and plowing services to his neighbors with his 1953 tractor.

Once a garage man, always a garage man, and Gary is still the consummate mechanic who never goes anywhere without his trusty adjustable wrench in his pocket. "It's come in handy many times over the years," he says, sometimes in surprising ways—like the time his wife dared him to get a tattoo. "Suddenly I found myself standing in a tattoo parlor with no idea what to have put on my arm until I reached my hand into my pocket and there was my trusty wrench." The surprised artist created a perfect rendering, and Gary was so pleased with the result that he had photos taken and sent them to his kids. "And do you know what?" he chuckles. "Not one of them has ever said a word about it. I'm sure they thought I was having a midlife crisis!"

"I always carry a wrench with me."

GLEN

When he began looking for a new home and base for his photography business, Glen gave his Realtor specific instructions: "Flat land in the mountains in a quiet, creative place." Soon after, a country store/gas station/garage/restaurant/bar, sitting high and alone on a mountain pass, appeared on the market. Glen grabbed it.

"It had great bones, but it needed love—a lot of love!" he says, rolling his eyes at the memory. "It was hard that first winter. I had no heat, no shower, and some of the walls were open to the sky. I'd work all day on the place and then I literally slept in my clothes and my boots, with Bob, my cat, for extra warmth."

But it's turned out to be just what Glen wanted. "It's ideal as a flexible, living work space because it's like one big garage inside. It can be a photo studio by day and a living space by night." And because, he says, "the ultimate recycling is re-use," most of the materials for the house have been salvaged—the wooden beams, spiral staircase, doors, cabinets, plant boxes, bricks, windows, and mirrors. The interior look is eclectic, totally original, and still evolving.

Glen hasn't yet gotten around to changing the exterior of the place, though. "I've kept the old gas station sign up for nostalgia, and it even still fools a few people. Just the other night, in the middle of a downpour and a thick fog, I heard a knock on the door and there stood a very wet motorcyclist looking for a cup of coffee and a place to get warm and dry. Of course, I obliged."

"I love the history of the building and its ties to the mountain community," Glen continues. "It was their social hub in the '70s and '80s—bar, restaurant, grocery store, dinner theater, bus stop, and mountain meeting place. Locals still come by and tell me stories about the wild parties that took place here," he laughs.

"It seems a million miles away, but it's only ten minutes to downtown and the beach." Standing in his completely secluded (former) parking lot, where the pine trees are his only neighbors, he jokes, "I haven't decided where the bathtub will go yet . . . it could be right here!"

"One man's garage is another man's house."

LYNN

The first time you walk into Lynn's suburban garage, you might think you have stepped into a real vintage race-car museum, with its ten Shelby Cobras, three hot rods, and a dragster all sitting handsomely on a carpeted floor and Cobra memorabilia everywhere. But if you think this magnificent collection is just for show, then you just don't know the man. Lynn will tell you, "We don't baby our cars—we drive them!"

For Lynn, driving the cars is a family affair. He and his wife love getting together with like-minded couples to tour in their Cobras. According to Lynn, "The girls love it and the guys love it, and everybody has a great time!" But he really gets the thrill of putting the pedal to the metal when he and his two sons hit California's vintage race-car circuit, driving at places like Laguna Seca near Monterey and Sonoma's Sears Point raceway.

As for all that Cobra memorabilia, Lynn confesses, "I'm a clutter bug by nature." His collection includes all manner of Cobra-related objects and souvenirs, and it continues to grow as fans keep sending him Cobra-themed things for his amusement—like the actual cobra snake in a wine bottle. "That caused a sensation in a restaurant when I asked the waitress to open it!" laughs Lynn.

Lynn's passion for cars goes way back. He says he can't even remember a time when he wasn't tinkering with cars and fixing engines, starting with Fords when he was a kid. Then, in 1962 a man named Carroll Shelby designed an automobile that combined Ford's high-performance engines with the stylish racing bodies of English cars, and Lynn's dream car was born. He bought his first Cobra that very year. But eight years later, when Lynn and his wife needed a down payment on a house, he decided to sell the car. It wasn't the Cobra lover's catastrophe it might have been, though, because as Lynn explains, "I had bought a wrecked Cobra that I could fix up," so he had a backup in place. Then he adds proudly, "That means I've owned at least one Cobra since 1962."

Of course, he's now added to his Shelby Cobra collection—nine, to be exact. And since only a thousand of these cars were ever made, having ten of them under one garage roof is pretty impressive.

"It's not about the cars—

it's about the people!"

MOE

"I've always loved movies with plenty of sword fighting," says Moe. "Ever since I was a little kid, I've been mesmerized by gladiators and medieval knights and dreamed that one day I'd have my own suit of armor. I just never thought I'd end up making it myself!" But that's exactly what he did fifteen years ago, right here in his garage.

Moe took his first step toward his dream when, at the age of seventeen, he spent a year as an apprentice to a professional armorer. If that sounds anachronistic, it might be because Moe himself is a bit of an anachronism, with one Nike-clad foot set solidly in the twenty-first century and the other metaled one somewhere back in medieval times. It's a way of life for him—he's an active member of the Society for Creative Anachronism, an international organization dedicated to researching and re-creating the arts and skills of pre-seventeenth-

"My garage is a creative place for me."

century Europe. That means that the armor not only looks good, but, as Moe says, "It's also fully functional combat armor."

Moe's armor is a hybrid design featuring early Roman-style shoulder plates and a late German chest plate. And although it looks like it's made out of beaten iron—a look that Moe has perfected over the years—it's actually made from aluminum and is very lightweight. "One of the advantages of designing and building your own armor in the twenty-first century," he says, "is you can make it comfortable to wear." According to Moe, "Modern armor is intended to fend off only wooden swords. Traditional armor would protect against a steel blade but could weigh between fifty and a hundred pounds." Then he laughs, "Those guys were tough back then."

Would he like to have lived in those days? "No," says Moe emphatically. "Although I'm attracted to the romance of the medieval period and the sense of honor and style attached to it, I'm sure that as a fighting man, or any man back in those times, I would have died very young—a horrible death, no doubt. There's no 'second place' in battle!"

Moe's metalworking and welding skills have led him into other areas of creativity as well, like jewelry and buckle design. "The guys at the local hardware store think I'm mad when I tell them what I'm welding together these days," he says. "But my skills have taught me to think out of the box."

JIM H.

Back in 1967, when Jim started building his train, he was fifty-two years old and conceived the undertaking as a leisurely hobby, a fun project to keep his precision metalworking skills fine-tuned through retirement. And that's exactly what his project turned out to be—leisurely—because forty years later Jim's still working on it.

Jim's train is a faithful one-eighth-scale replica of the 2,000- to 3,000-horsepower Rio Grande Pacific locomotive that ran in the early part of the twentieth century. He points out that his train has a "leading truck" and "trailing truck," steam engine innovations that, according to Jim, made it possible to keep the enormous driving wheels on a curving track. As he puts it, "Wheels need to be statically balanced, especially the driving wheels, where horizontal motion is transferred to circular motion." And when he talks about energy transference, there is a special twinkle in his eye: this is Jim's forte—he's a gear man.

His garage is filled with all manner of metalworking equipment, from simple metal lathes to gigantic optical machines that can cut metal with a precision of one-tenth of one-thousandth of an inch—in layman's terms, this is a machine that can slice the width of a human hair into five strands. And in this garage Jim has crafted gears for just about everything, from MG sports cars to rockets, because, he says, "Even in the electronic age, spacecraft need gears." At this very moment, somewhere in the solar system, Jim's gears are whirring through space, transferring energy into motion, the perfect marriage of Newtonian physics and human ingenuity.

Back on Earth, Jim's five-hundred-pound train remains firmly rooted on a very short track in his garage, though he says he can finally foresee the day when the boilers will get up a head of steam and pistons will drive the wheels of his magnificent locomotive. He just hasn't got an exact date in mind yet.

In his ninety-two years, Jim has seen the world move from steam engines to rockets, from terra firma to outer space, and he's been on board for every minute of it. For Jim, it's all about the journey.

"I'm a gear man."

ABOUT THE AUTHOR

Helena Day Breese grew up in England and now makes her home in California.

Long intrigued by the pleasure British men find pottering about in their "sheds," she has taken her curiosity and her camera on the road to explore the American equivalent of this male sanctuary in **Guys and Garages**.

To learn more about the guys and their garages, visit www.guysandgarages.com.